LEAVING ACADEMIA

Leaving Academia

A Practical Guide

Christopher L. Caterine

PRINCETON UNIVERSITY PRESS

PRINCETON AND OXFORD

Requests for permission to reproduce material from this work
should be sent to permissions@press.princeton.edu

Published by Princeton University Press
41 William Street, Princeton, New Jersey 08540
6 Oxford Street, Woodstock, Oxfordshire OX20 1TR

press.princeton.edu

ISBN 9780691200200
ISBN (pbk.) 9780691200194
ISBN (e-book) 9780691209869

Library of Congress Control Number: 2020940409

British Library Cataloging-in-Publication Data is available

Editorial: Peter Dougherty and Alena Chekanov
Production Editorial: Karen Carter
Jacket/Cover Design: Layla Mac Rory
Production: Erin Suydam
Publicity: Kate Farquhar-Thomson and Alyssa Sanford
Copyeditor: Aviva Arad

This book has been composed in Adobe Text and Gotham

Printed on acid-free paper. ∞

Printed in the United States of America

10 9 8 7 6 5 4 3 2 1

For Mallory

Let's keep being tired for the right reasons

CONTENTS

PREFACE

Leaving academia is hard. It's not just that you face the psychological hurdle of giving up a field you've come to see as a vocation. You also have to contend with the debt, low pay, and lack of benefits that follow most people for the first decade or more that they work as professional scholars. These facts can make the risk of seeking a new career—and of building the skills it requires—seem unacceptably large. Many academics consequently choose to stay put rather than pursue new work that can bring them more satisfaction, stability, or savings.

Let me put my cards on the table. I was luckier than most when I decided the challenges I was certain to face within higher education were scarier than what I might face in the world beyond it. I'd grown up in a wealthy home, attended schools that groomed me for the modern professional world, and learned how to behave by watching adults who were active parts of it. This experience meant that from an early age I was familiar with what work looks like in modern nonacademic professions. More than that, I knew many people—friends, parents, mentors—whom I could call on for help. It was a great benefit to never doubt that they could or would come to my aid. Even greater was not having to wonder whether I could fit in once I landed a corporate job.

Yet even for me, leaving academia was hard. It took over two years and meetings with more than 150 people before I found a job. I spent most of that time feeling my way through the dark. Although I read what resources I could, I was often unable to put their advice into context or see how it contributed to a larger strategy for changing careers.

I've written this book so that those without direct access to the privileges I had can still benefit from the lessons they afforded me. Most of all I was blessed with time. I held a "good" visiting assistant professorship that only carried a 3–3 teaching load, I had two years left on my contract when I decided to explore other options, and I had a wife whose salary could support me—at least for a time—if I faced unemployment. Those safety nets allowed me to run down rabbit holes and make mistakes. They also let me reflect on my experiences. A blog that chronicled my explorations helped me realize my potential as a writer. That project led not only to this book, but also to the professional work I've done since 2017.

ACKNOWLEDGMENTS

It was only in January 2018 that I thought to turn my experiences into a personal report and practical guide for others contemplating a move out of higher education. At the time I was just four months past my career in academia and still very much new to the world beyond it. My friends Mali and Raf nevertheless saw potential in my blog and encouraged me to revise those posts for a longer project. My first debt of gratitude is to them: without their encouragement, I never would have taken this project on.

I'd also like to thank the former academics I interviewed while expanding and revising my initial draft. They didn't just give me their time, but granted permission to tell their tales alongside my own. To Chela White-Ramsey, Chris Papadopoulos, David Engel, David Stevens, Kristi Lodge, Laura Ansley, Liz Segran, Patricia Soler, Susanne Cohen, Vay Cao, and my anonymous anthropologist: Thank you! I know from comparing the before and after that you've made this book infinitely more useful to others who are undertaking the transition we did.

Mike Zimm deserves special acknowledgment among this group. Beyond lending me his story, he's been a steadfast friend and sounding board throughout my career transition and adjustment to life outside higher education.

Dan Porterfield was the first person I spoke with about leaving academia. His advice and encouragement set me on the path to a new career when I was utterly at a loss about how to proceed. He also allowed me to share the details of that conversation at the start of chapter 3—and provided further guidance as I prepared my final draft for publication.

When I quietly began exploring other fields in 2015, Susann Lusnia connected me to administrators at Tulane and Loyola University in New Orleans—meetings that served as my first foray into informational interviews and networking.

Andrew Foley showed me that academics can find intellectual satisfaction in a business setting and allowed me to share the story of how we met.

My editor, Peter Dougherty, enabled me to transform the very short and rough manuscript that crossed his desk in January 2019 into a stronger, more serious book of guidance. In every matter he has been attentive, patient, and helpful. Most of all, I owe him thanks for allowing me to achieve an accomplishment I thought was beyond reach after I left academia: publishing a book with a university press.

In 2018, John Paulas organized a networking event for nonacademic careers at the Society for Classical Studies' annual conference. That occasion was the first time I advised others on leaving the professoriate. John later introduced me to some of the professionals I interviewed while revising this book and agreed (although at first secretly) to serve as one of its reviewers. In the latter role he gave keen advice, particularly in identifying best practices I initially overlooked.

Even if Lenny Cassuto hadn't taken a principled stand against "double-blind" review by sneaking his name into his report on my first draft of this book, it would be an understatement to call him "Reader 2." He was a critic in the truest sense of the word, discerning infelicities and inconsistencies in my tone, meaning, and argumentation—and articulating them in a manner that allowed me to attempt a remedy. I was humbled by how much time he committed to reading two drafts of my manuscript, and am especially grateful for the extensive handwritten notes he provided to improve my prose style in September 2019. It's not hyperbole to say this book would be far worse without Lenny's extraordinary interventions. His honesty, seriousness, and generosity touched every page—and reminded me what academic exchange can be when it is at its very best.

Ariane Schwartz has become a trusted friend and advisor, though ironically only since we both left classics for consulting. I owe her thanks for her feedback on my second draft, as well as for her expertise as we collaborated on a presentation to help graduate departments prepare students for a variety of careers in January 2020.

Chris Humphrey and Jen Polk helped me widen this book's appeal beyond the US market by identifying places where I had been overly American in my thinking or diction.

Adam McCune, Coleman Connelly, and Jon MacLellan "test-drove" my advice and provided feedback during their own career transitions.

Donna Zuckerberg has been an immense support throughout this project, volunteering her editorial eye whenever I hit a roadblock and providing guidance when I began to strategize the book's release. More importantly, her friendship has been a constant gift since our earliest days of grad school.

I also owe thanks to the many people I met in New Orleans and beyond as I felt my way to a new career. It's not just that this vast network enabled me to succeed. Their advice permeates this book so fully that it would be impossible to give credit in every instance.

My mom and dad never questioned my decision to enter academia. Nor did they ever question my decision to leave it. Throughout both phases of my life they offered love and support—and listened to me talk through my doubts, excitements, and fears with a patience that I've only begun to appreciate since having a son of my own.

My deepest gratitude belongs to my wife, Mallory. She stood with me through the darkest days of my career transition, tolerated more than her share of discussions about how I might proceed, and adapted to a radically different lifestyle when I found a job that keeps me on the road for a third of each year. Once this book was underway, she endured my tunnel vision in the thick of writing and encouraged me when I dragged my heels. It's incredible to me that she provided this support at all, let alone that she did so through the pregnancy, birth, and infancy of our son Caleb; while advancing her career at Tulane; and amid her successful launch of Kallion, a nonprofit to elevate leadership through the humanities. For the countless ways in which my life is better for having her at its center, it's to her that I dedicate this volume.

LEAVING ACADEMIA

1

Dread

Confidence is where this story begins. It was confidence to me, at any rate—though others might have called it arrogance. That firm conviction I'd be successful. Not lucky, mind you. I believed academia was a meritocracy and trusted my ability to outthink, outwork, or outlast whatever stood between me and a professorship.

Confidence was good. Or at least it was good for me. Confidence got me up early to prepare for general exams. It let me stand in front of a classroom full of excitement and passion. It stoked a desire to leave grad school behind and pursue the next phase of my career. It drove me to write articles and revise thesis chapters for publication, albeit in a future that was always undefined.

Confidence was crushing. In truth, it's crushing to most. After three years on "the market," I finally realized academia *isn't* a meritocracy, my hard work *wasn't* coming to fruition, my career *wouldn't* be spent as a professor. There's a reason people talk about blind confidence. Anyone could have told me the numbers were never in my favor, but I refused to believe them. So there I was at thirty years old, caught unawares.

Confidence was gone. I felt hemmed in, pinned down, unsure of where to turn. The change was sudden—and radical, too. Shame, anxiety, and fear combined to weigh me down as much as confidence had buoyed me. Leaving academia had overwhelmed me with a potent new emotion: pure, unmitigated dread.

An Event Horizon

Graduate education is broken.[1] Most doctoral programs train their students to serve as tenure-track professors, but today only 7 percent of people who enter grad school in the United States will secure one of those coveted positions.[2] In this environment, we may safely say **there is no such thing as an "alt-ac" career: *academia* is the alternative path.**

Ironically, grad students, recent PhDs, and the people who advise them have responded to this state of affairs by digging in their heels: now more than ever, these groups view anything

book

1. Lenny Cassuto, *The Graduate School Mess* (2015), presents a detailed assessment of this situation, as well as advice for how faculty and administrators can address it. My own book offers more immediate aid to those impacted by "the mess."

2. This calculation is my own, and admittedly imperfect (see n. 6 for details). Lenny Cassuto (2015) notes that "data on overall Ph.D. academic job placement are too poor to support a data-driven graph" (p. 190); even so, he recently provided an estimate only marginally more optimistic than my own: "for every eight students who enter a humanities Ph.D. program, about four will not finish. . . . Of the four who do, statistically, two will eventually get full-time teaching jobs. Less than one will get a full-time job teaching at a research university" (quotation from Emma Pettit, "Columbia Had Little Success Placing English Ph.D.s on the Tenure Track. 'Alarm' Followed, and the University Responded," *Chronicle of Higher Education*, August 21, 2019: https://www.chronicle.com/article/Columbia-Had-Little-Success/246989).

besides total devotion to a field as a harbinger of failure.[3] It's yet to be seen whether initiatives to reverse this trend will succeed.[4]

For academics considering the world beyond higher education, the situation is akin to looking at a black hole. You know the object is there, but it's impossible to see past the event horizon that shrouds its true workings in mystery. Its gravitational pull actually makes that limit a point of no return: anything that moves beyond the event horizon is unable to cross back over again, at least not without being irrevocably and utterly transformed. These attributes make leaving academia awesome in the word's original sense: enormous and terrifying. Many people consequently try to keep even its event horizon in the distance—preferring the familiarity of the world they know to the risk and uncertainty of being drawn into a different career.

I've written this book after safely crossing that metaphorical limit. I was, in fact, transformed by the process: I'm now far happier than I ever was in academia.

Even so, I didn't achieve that state without my share of suffering. It took me over two years to expand my sense of what I could do, to develop new skills, to learn how to convey my strengths to those from other backgrounds—and finally to get a job. Along the way, I was plagued by doubt. I didn't just fear

3. L. Maren Wood, "Odds Are, Your Doctorate Will Not Prepare You for a Profession outside Academe," *Chronicle of Higher Education*, July 9, 2019: https://www.chronicle.com/article/Odds-Are-Your-Doctorate-Will/246613.

4. In 2018, the American Association of Universities started the PhD Education Initiative to "promote more student-centered doctoral education at AAU universities by making diverse PhD career pathways visible, valued, and viable." Eight institutions piloted this program in 2019, but no results had been quantified by the time of publication.

that leaving was the wrong choice. I also worried I could only ever be good at research and teaching. Fortunately, these concerns faded the more I learned about the world beyond academia. There was an added benefit of that exploration, too: for the first time in years, I had the feeling that there were more open doors before me than closed ones.

Background to the Book

This book distills the lessons I personally learned while changing careers, as well as advice I received from the roughly 150 people I met while leaving academia. The latter group is diverse. It spans businesspeople, nonprofit directors, college administrators, civil servants, and other trained professionals.

I've supplemented their wisdom with formal interviews of twelve former academics (listed on page 5). These individuals come from different backgrounds, trained in different disciplines, and have gone into different professions. While I initially collected their stories as a check on my experience, I found time and again that their stories were remarkably similar to my own. Regardless of our discipline and eventual career, academics who succeed beyond the professoriate become good at meeting new people, taking risks, and learning from every experience— whether good or bad.

I never imagined these traits might describe me when I began my career transition. As an academic, my chief professional goal was to become the leading expert on a minor Roman poet. I was an introvert—and proud of it. I didn't have many hobbies, and as you'll read in chapter 3, I thought that made me more credible in the role I aspired to.

Change took time. It wasn't natural for me to reach out to strangers, ask them for help, or accept the challenges they

Name	Current Role, Employer*	Academic Field, School	Degree (Year)
Laura Ansley	Managing Editor, American Historical Association	History, the College of William and Mary	MA (2012), ABD
Vania Cao	Asia Pacific Sales Manager and Support Lead, Inscopix	Neuroscience, Brown University	PhD (2013)
Susanne Cohen	Principal UX Researcher, Elsevier	Anthropology, University of Michigan	PhD (2010)
David Engel	Managing Director, Wells Fargo Advisors	Philosophy, University of California at Berkeley	PhD (1997)
Kristine Lodge	Graduate Career Advisor, University of Oregon Lundquist College of Business	Medieval Studies, University of Oregon	PhD (2010)
Chris Papadopoulos	Data Scientist, Credit Karma	Physics, University of Maryland	PhD (2009)
Elizabeth Segran	Senior Staff Writer, *Fast Company Magazine;* Author of *The Rocket Years: How Your Twenties Launch the Rest of Your Life*	Southeast Asian Studies, University of California at Berkeley	PhD (2011)
Patricia Soler	IT Specialist, US Department of Housing and Urban Development	Latin American Studies, Georgetown University	PhD (2014)
David Stevens	Founding Partner and acting CEO of Broaden By WPI	Politics, Princeton University	MA (2006), ABD
Chela White-Ramsey	Senior Training and Development Manager, Indeed, Inc.	Human Resource Leadership, Louisiana State University	PhD (2015)
Michael Zimm	Director of Marketing, Kris-Tech Wire	Classics (history focus), Yale University	PhD (2016)
Anonymous	Top 3 Technology Firm	Anthropology, Ivy League University	PhD (2016)

* As of February 2020

offered. But these activities provided a path forward when I desperately needed one. So I fought through the discomfort and made myself do them.

Practice hardened these efforts into habits. I gradually realized that even silly opportunities presented a chance to learn, and that each new experience brought me closer to whatever career my future held. As that happened, the world beyond academia became less and less scary, because by then it was actually familiar.

Everyone reading this book will already possess at least one of the traits you need to change careers successfully. Your academic training has made you curious and critical, instilling a reflex to consider not just what's right or wrong about your work, but *why*. That impulse defines people with our background and runs like a thread through every career transition I've heard about over the last five years. Crucially, this trait will enable you to acquire the others—and so to find a new career outside the academy.

Intended Audience

I've written *Leaving Academia* for grad students, recent PhDs, and professors who've grown dissatisfied with their prospects in higher education.[5] My hope is that reading it will make your path easier as you venture beyond the ivory tower.

I know how hard leaving can be because I was once in your shoes: a visiting assistant professor of Roman history and Latin literature with virtually no knowledge of what nonacademic jobs entailed. I was scared at how large the rest of the world

---

5. Throughout this book I refer to these groups interchangeably, a choice I've made for the sake of lexical variety rather than because of ignorance of the differences between them. I also expect some readers will be committed members of the professoriate who want to provide their students better advice.

appeared—and I was daunted by my ignorance of who else had ventured into it.

There are three ways people find themselves where you are now: academic roadblocks, personal causes external to your work, and professional changes of heart.

Academic roadblocks are work-related disappointments that compel you to seek a new career. Most of you will know these challenges all too well: the bleak job market, program cuts, failed tenure reviews, and the like. Since these events are tied to your field and professional identity, leaving academia because of them can feel like an indictment of your professional capabilities.

Let me disabuse you of this belief. Today in the United States, only about 1.2 percent of people who enter a doctoral program in the arts and humanities earn a tenure-track position at a leading institution.[6] The situation isn't much better if you remove that final qualifier. People in *any* tenure-track job represent just 2–7 percent of those who start a PhD. To state the case inversely, **more than nine out of ten academics don't achieve the career most of us hoped for** when we set down the path to an advanced degree. I never expected to find comfort in

---

6. I had to use multiple statistical studies of higher ed to arrive at this number. Given slight differences in their time frames and how they grouped disciplines, my calculation can only be taken as a rough estimate. In particular, I multiplied out the following figures:

43 percent of doctoral students in the humanities actually finish their degree (National Academies of Science, Engineering, and Medicine. 2011. "Data-Based Assessment of Research-Doctorate Programs in the United States.")

56 percent of *employed* humanities PhDs in 2015 were teaching at the postsecondary level (Humanities Indicators. 2018. "Indicator III-7a.")

27 percent of faculty jobs in 2018 are tenured or tenure track (American Association of University Professors. 2018. "Data Snapshot: Contingent Faculty in US Higher Ed.")

19 percent of history PhDs worked at R1 institutions in 2017 (American Historical Association. 2018. "Where Historians Work.")

statistics, but those numbers stopped me in my tracks.[7] People don't succeed or fail at being academics in this kind of market: they simply fall victim to luck.

Some people decide to play the academic odds anyway. For those who do, the situation is bleak. The American Association of University Professors (AAUP) recently reported that 73 percent of college professors work as adjuncts—that is, in contingent roles with semesterly contracts, limited job security, and unreliable access to benefits like health insurance. A quarter of this group is enrolled in public assistance programs. Many more qualify.[8] There is no shame in wanting to avoid or escape a career that provides so little material support: leaving academia under these circumstances may even come as a relief.

The numerical consolations I've offered thus far may ring hollow if the roadblock that prevents you from an academic career is the behavior of a colleague. Harassment and inappropriate actions stemming from sexism, racism, ableism, and the like can drive talented people from their fields and keep underrepresented groups from establishing the footholds they deserve. None of that is fair, and I can only imagine how suffering bias would tempt many people to fight for change. I wish the best of luck to those who try. As for those who are ready to cut bait, my sincere hope is that this book will help you find a more supportive profession as quickly as possible.

---

7. For a fuller discussion of these trends and additional insights on how women and minorities are especially harmed by them, see the introduction to Joseph Fruscione and Kelly Baker's 2018 book, *Succeeding Outside the Academy*.

8. Ken Jacobs, Ian Perry, and Jenifer MacGillvary, "The High Public Cost of Low Wages: Poverty-Level Wages Cost U.S. Taxpayers $152.8 Billion Each Year in Public Support for Working Families" (research brief, 2015): http://laborcenter.berkeley.edu/pdf/2015/the-high-public-cost-of-low-wages.pdf.

Others leave academia because of personal causes external to their work, such as illness, pregnancy, and family exigencies. These situations can take a considerable toll: circumstances are already stressful, and leaving a field you love compounds the difficulty. Even so, it is hard (or at least uncharitable) to interpret a career change undertaken for these reasons as a professional failure. Life can throw anyone a curve ball.

Being in this group offers at least one consolation: it's easy to explain why you're seeking a new profession. Employers are people, too, and many will sympathize with the challenging circumstances that led you to change careers instead of questioning why you left a job most assume is your passion.

The last reason you might abandon higher education is a professional change of heart—that is, you realize you don't want to work in the sector any longer. Even if most academics don't discuss this occurrence openly, it's a perfectly normal experience. It can happen because you lose interest in your research, tire of the publish-or-perish rat race, or desire new and different experiences than you can have in higher education. If you hit a plateau or come to see the professoriate as a bad occupation, it's likely time to explore alternative lines of work.

Of course, these factors aren't mutually exclusive. Many of you may feel a variety of them shaping your decision. And if you're anything like me, you may realize in a few years that the last one exerted a far greater sway than you're willing to admit right now.

The Vocation Trap

Whatever led you to seek a new career, you're embarking on a challenging journey. In its course you'll experience major changes in three areas of your personal identity:

1. How you view yourself
2. How other people view you
3. How you interact with the world around you

Many academics—I'd even venture to say most—find it hard to embrace change in these specific areas. As a group, we tend to view our work in higher education as more than a career: we consider it a vocation. The doubts we're prone to feel as we think about working in a different sector thus go beyond the practicalities of not knowing what it's like to do a new job. In a very real way, we worry that we don't know *who we'll be* if we cease to be academics.

When this anxiety collides with the realities discussed in the last section, it can trigger an unhealthy spiral of emotions. I raged at the cruelties of the job market, faulted advisors for not making me a more attractive candidate, and loathed the ABDs who beat me out for jobs. Most of all, I blamed myself for not working hard enough or on the right topics to become a tenure-track professor.

These feelings were clearly misdirected, but I don't blame myself for indulging them. If you're a "true believer" in the academic mission, it's natural to struggle as you come to terms with changing careers. The situation is akin to a breakup. You invested years in a discipline because you liked it and cared about it. Recognizing that your love will go unrequited is going to hurt—even in the best of circumstances. The challenge is that if you get caught in that spiral of emotions, fear of the unknown can prevent you from being willing to move on.

I'd like to give you two reasons to resist that urge. First, the risk of *not* changing careers is both real and significant. I mentioned above that contingent positions now make up about 73 percent of faculty jobs, and that one quarter of adjuncts in the United States are recipients of public assistance. Shocking as those statistics may be, they don't adequately convey the burdens of contingent life. Its demands have driven some people to work themselves to death. Literally.[9]

In April 2019, Adam Harris of *The Atlantic* told the story of Thea Hunter.[10] She earned her PhD in history from Columbia University and held a few good temporary positions after finishing. As time went on, she had to cobble together full-time teaching as an adjunct at multiple institutions. She worked hard, but each college viewed her as part-time faculty. That determination meant she wasn't eligible for health insurance, and when her lungs started hurting, she had no way to see a doctor. She consequently treated the pain the way she'd always treated asthma. Before she or anyone else could realize how severe the illness was, it robbed her of her life.

For all that this story marks an extreme in the adjunct experience, it reflects a wider reality: day-to-day life is exceptionally hard for the majority of people who try to make it as a professor. At least for me, the fear of doing something else, and indeed of becoming *someone* else, was ultimately smaller than the dread I experienced staring into that personal and professional abyss.

My second argument against letting fear keep you in academia is perhaps better called a reassurance: while the sting of leaving a career you love is sharp, and it may be hard to imagine it getting better, the pain of disappointment *will* eventually fade. Nearly every former academic I interviewed for this book

9. American Association of University Professors. 2018. "Data Snapshot: Contingent Faculty in US Higher Ed."

10. Adam Harris, "The Death of an Adjunct," *The Atlantic,* April 8, 2015: https://www.theatlantic.com/education/archive/2019/04/adjunct-professors-higher-education-thea-hunter/586168/.

assured me of this fact, as did those I met during my own career change. I can now confirm it myself.

One way to accelerate that process is to salve the wound. I discovered an unlikely balm just two months into my career search. I was sitting at my computer, skimming job requirements and fretting about how much they differed from academic listings. Then a thought dawned on me: no matter what job I ended up getting, no matter how bad or embarrassing it was, I would never have to read German scholarship in order to do it.

This realization came as a great relief. Despite years of practice, I had always viewed tasks involving German as a chore: I delayed my proficiency exam as long as I could in grad school, and my research process intentionally tackled articles in English, Italian, and French before reading *auf Deutsch*. So I wasn't surprised when my lips turned upward at the thought of never reading German again. But this uncontrollable response sparked another epiphany that *did* catch me off guard: I was smiling at the thought of not being a professor.

User's Guide

As its subtitle states, this book is meant as a practical guide. Its six chapters will escort you from the dread many experience when considering work outside the professoriate through the period when you adapt to your first nonacademic job.

Each chapter covers a different phase in this journey, using an event from my own career transition—and an assessment of how I handled it—to kick off more general advice. These discussions begin with three questions you'll answer about yourself and your career as you move through a given phase. While not exhaustive, they can focus your thoughts more clearly and assist you in diagnosing where to invest the greatest effort. Each chapter then continues with advice, anecdotes, and practical steps to help you move closer to a satisfying career beyond academia. I end each chapter with three action items to help you start putting my guidance into practice.

I've arranged this material so you can read it all at once, go chapter by chapter, or flit between sections that interest you. My aim was to keep these units short and the volume user-friendly.

Further Reading and Other Resources

The guidance I give throughout *Leaving Academia* is meant to be exhaustive enough that you can successfully change careers even if it's the only book you read on the subject. But other resources are available, including how-to guides, debriefs with former academics, "quit lit," communities of job seekers, and even coaches who advise people on leaving higher ed for greener pastures.

I recommend using this volume as a starting point. After reading it, you'll possess a benchmark of best practices for your career transition that will enable you to derive greater value from any specialized resources you consult. A brief survey will help you navigate that sea of material if or when you decide to do so.

The standard book for the last generation has been *So What Are You Going to Do with That?* by Susan Basalla and Maggie *book* Debelius, now in its third edition. It remains a rich source of material on landing a career outside academia, particularly as it breaks down the mechanics of refashioning yourself for a new job market. *So What* is also remarkable for the array of anecdotes it collects from people who have successfully turned away from scholarship to embrace a new profession. Are you seeking an example of someone with your specific degree who changed careers? Odds are this book has one.

The downside of this approach is that *So What*'s plethora of stories prevents you from seeing any one in significant detail. For me, that meant learning a lot about *what* to do, but far less about *how* to do it. A range of questions that felt essential were simply left unanswered: How did a person first encounter a challenge, where did they suffer doubts, how did they overcome them?

In short, *So What* gives you the impression that anything is possible for a PhD. That's very much to its credit. But the step-by-step process it sets forth doesn't always dig into the habits and ways of thinking that to my mind make changing careers so hard for academics in the first place.

A book that addresses this concern more effectively is Joseph Fruscione and Kelly Baker's *Succeeding Outside the Academy*. This volume groups fourteen ten-page essays by former academics into two categories: (1) "Reconsidering Academic Careers and Success"; and (2) "Creating New Careers." In comparison to *So What*, these retrospectives tell more complete stories—and strike an admirable balance between sympathizing with people in your shoes and synthesizing lessons from the authors' journeys beyond the academy.

Even so, *Succeeding* has its flaws. Chief among them is lack of cohesion. Although the book's stories are illustrative and compelling, they don't hold together as a unified work—no doubt because different people wrote them. A second (and more problematic) issue is that readers may struggle to know when to consult a given chapter. *Succeeding* doesn't depict a career transition in broad outline, and the two categories the editors use to divide its essays are insufficiently precise. While these deficiencies don't undo the book's merits, they make it more suitable as a secondary resource than as a general guide.

Inside Higher Ed, the *Chronicle of Higher Education*, and other publications also house articles about leaving academia. These opinion pieces vary in quality, running the gamut from "quit lit" to more thoughtful statements of practical advice. While some may offer specialized help that you find useful, they were always most valuable to me as a breath of fresh air when I felt like I was drowning.

In 2017, panic was setting in as I entered the last semester of my teaching contract. I was still far from finding a nonacademic job, and I had less than six months until my last paycheck. Michael Zimm's "From Homer to High Tech" appeared as a godsend.[11] The article didn't just provide practical ideas to move my career search forward, it also helped me keep the fear of unemployment at bay. I was so struck by Mike's advice that I soon decided to contact him. As you'll read later, that decision led indirectly to my new career—and won me a close friend.

Online communities of "academic refugees" are another resource you can use to accelerate your departure from higher education.[12] These groups can connect you to new people, industries, and opportunities regardless of where you live. Most useful are those populated by members from your academic disciplines: they will understand the specific challenges of your transition and can provide a clearer glimpse into what work looks like after you shed your scholarly identity.

11. Michael Zimm, "From Homer to High Tech," *Chronicle of Higher Education*, January 23, 2017: https://www.chronicle.com/article/From-Homer-to-High-Tech /238982.

12. I should state here that I've yet to read or coin a term that I actually like for former academics.

These communities include businesses that specialize in transitioning academics to satisfying careers in other sectors. While space doesn't allow a comprehensive list, I've highlighted a few to provide you with a starting point:[13]

- Academics Mean Business
- Beyond the Professoriate
- Free the PhD
- IncipitCareer — *Kristi Lodge , U of O*
- Imagine PhD
- Jobs on Toast
- PhD Matters
- The Professor Is In
- The Versatile PhD

As diverse as online groups may be, their variety pales in comparison to what's on social media. Twitter, LinkedIn, and Facebook offer a constant stream of reflections, advice, and complaints that can help you at every step of your transition. The catch is that these forums lack structure. They may provide good treatments of discrete topics, but there's no single place where you can find them—let alone any way to put them into a sensible order. The result? It's easy to get overwhelmed by the torrent of information. By all means dip your toe in that river if you're looking for additional advice, but use this book to secure your footing first.

13. I have ties to many of these organizations. I wrote a guest blog post for Beyond the Professoriate about aligning your life and career goals, and cofounder Jen Polk read a draft of this book. Kristi Lodge of IncipitCareers and Vania Cao of Free the PhD are two of the people I interviewed while writing. John Paulas of PhD Matters was one of my readers and leads a networking event at the annual meeting of the Society for Classical Studies that I have attended since its inception. Chris Humphrey of *Jobs on Toast* advised me on making my advice relevant to a UK audience.

Caveat Lector (Reader Beware)

My advice isn't a cure-all. I've collected guidance that I believe
will help you find a new career that makes you happy, but some
people accomplish this end more easily than others. The time
you invest, the people you meet, and your emotional bond
to your discipline all have an impact on the outcome. And
although your personal disposition will evolve as you change
careers, it will nevertheless influence your feelings about leaving academia as you find your way to a new path.

David Engel stands at one extreme. All he ever wanted to be
was a scholar, all he'd ever trained to be was a scholar, and the
only thing he thought he was capable of being was a scholar.
But the realities of being a professional philosopher wore him
down. Four years into a tenure-track job, he didn't have hobbies, grew disillusioned with the cult of personality that sur-
rounded successful teachers, and spent hours every weekend
driving to see his wife in another city.

It was 2001 when she told him, in a matter-of-fact way, that
he was unhappy. At first he dismissed her assessment. But on
his drive home that Sunday afternoon, as his dog leaned forward from the back seat and rested its head on his shoulder for
a scratch, he came around to seeing she was right.

David still struggled with his decision to leave. He felt like
a fraud for abandoning his field—and he'd quit his job without
a plan. But unemployment didn't last long. David remarkably
transformed a data-entry job from a temp agency into a permanent position at a bank. He then worked his way to the top of
his field, now serving as a managing director with Wells Fargo
Advisors.

Despite achieving unqualified success in his new career, it's
been hard for David to shake the feelings of embarrassment

and fear he experienced when leaving academia. A few years ago, when he was already doing quite well, his wife caught him lingering by the shelves they'd installed for his old academic books. "You're doing it again," she said, "you're saying you're a failure." Once again, her assessment was correct. A decade had passed since he had written his last academic article, yet David still felt a lingering sadness.

To be clear, this doesn't mean he dislikes his job or regrets his departure from academia. Quite the opposite! But like so many of us, David embraced scholarship as a vocation and built up being an academic into the single defining element of his identity. Hindsight has taught him that this was a mistake—and that his attitudes towards work made a career change harder than it had to be.

A colleague of mine had an entirely different experience. Despite spending more than ten years in academia, he instantly fell for the speed, challenge, and compensation of business. He misses almost nothing of the day-to-day life he lived as a professor. In fact, an Ivy League school invited him to interview for a tenure-track job less than three months after he started his role in consulting. He didn't even make time to discuss it: once he'd seen what life could be like, going back to academia became unthinkable.

These stories won't be exact reflections of your experience—and aren't meant to be. Instead, they represent two extremes of the emotional spectrum you'll occupy when you give up a career you consider a vocation. They also teach a useful lesson: however attached you may be to your life as an academic, you can find even greater satisfaction and joy by pursuing another career.

That last reassurance isn't a platitude: there's research to back it up. In 2018, the Cornell Higher Education Research

Institute released a working paper that detailed how PhDs outside academia report higher levels of job satisfaction than their
counterparts in the professoriate.[14] One element of their findings may give you special solace: a greater degree of happiness
still held for those who left their fields unwillingly.

Light at the End of the Tunnel

Liz Segran has this conversation often. Since trading academia
for journalism, she's come to appreciate that leaving your discipline is necessarily difficult—and that your situation usually
gets harder before it gets better. The trouble is that anticipating
challenges often prevents people from embracing a new career,
leaving them trapped in a cycle of temporary academic work.

Liz is keen to remind those in your position that your outlook will get better in the long run. You already possess skills
that average people don't have, such as writing, researching,
and analytical abilities. What you usually lack is knowledge of
a particular subject matter or work environment. Once you
acquire that experience, you become a valuable asset in the
marketplace and can advance more rapidly than your peers.

The challenge, of course, is overcoming the hurdles that
stand between you and that new knowledge. Many academics stumble because they don't start out where they want to in
their first job beyond the professoriate. Some dislike having to

14. Joyce B. Main, Sarah Prenovitz, and Ronald G. Ehrenberg, "In Pursuit of a
Tenure-Track Faculty Position: Career Progression and Satisfaction of Humanities
and Social Sciences Doctorates" (working paper, 2018): https://www.ilr.cornell.edu
/sites/default/files/CHERI%20WP180.pdf. See also Colleen Flaherty's report on the
working paper for *Inside Higher Ed*, December 18, 2017: https://www.insidehighered
.com/news/2017/12/18/study-humanities-and-social-science-phds-working-outside
-academe-are-happier-their.

ask questions (that is, they chafe against not being an expert). Others resist being a thirty-year-old intern with twenty-one-year-old "peers." Sometimes a nine to five routine is boring or workplace dynamics feel alien to what passes for normal in academia. It doesn't matter who you are or what you do: everyone finds *something* unpleasant about changing careers.

Enduring that "something" is nevertheless essential to developing the knowledge or skills that will enable your future success. Once you settle into your new environment, your situation will rapidly improve. You'll connect dots faster, synthesize information with greater ease, and explain complex topics more clearly than people who have more experience but less formal training in the art of learning. Your new colleagues will recognize these abilities, and most will come to appreciate the skills you honed through years of grad school. Competence, intelligence, and drive are always in vogue.

So fight the urge to give in to fear: you have less to lose from changing careers than you might think, and quite a lot more that you can gain.

While you may not be able to imagine the benefits of leaving academia now, they're decidedly both real and tangible. To name an obvious one first: the salaries are often higher. After so many years living on a paltry income, it's a relief to know you can cover a surprise expense—and that you won't be expected to pay your way to a required conference or absorb the cost of a cross-country move. In time, changing careers also removes the effort of constant applications, the fear of living apart from friends or family, and the often-crushing burden of putting your life on hold.

It's also liberating to disentangle your ego from your work. When I first entered academia, I wanted to shape young minds and change how future scholars interpreted Roman literature.

That made my work feel important—and gave me a sense of meaning. But my day-to-day efforts rarely mapped onto those lofty goals. Instead, I spent a decade trying to inflect a scholarly discussion with a global audience of fifty and forcing college students to memorize details of Latin grammar.

Today, I get far more satisfaction committing my time, treasure, and talent to other pursuits. My job is just that: a way of supporting myself. I enjoy it immensely and take pride in doing good work, but don't delude myself into thinking it's the entirety of who I am, or that it must have philosophical significance to be worth the effort.

In fact, I've been surprised to find that working in business allows me to support communities and causes I care about much more than I could in academia. I can afford to make larger, more regular donations to these groups—and my new experience has made me more capable of advising them on how to advance their mission and maximize their impact. Whenever I rehash questions of my work's philosophical significance, it's clear that, on balance, my new career puts me far ahead.

A Wide World of Work

Many industries thriving today—such as information technology, data science, and medicine—present viable careers for people with advanced degrees. Although these stalwarts of the knowledge-based economy pursue pragmatic rather than cerebral ends, they often emerged from higher education and retain certain cultural ties to that world.

Work in these fields may consequently feel more familiar than you expect. As in academia, you'll grapple with complex problems, synthesize data from diverse areas, and develop innovative solutions. The chief difference is the measure of

outcomes

success: results in addressing human problems. Many of the people I interviewed were nevertheless quick to add a second, more pragmatic divergence: delivering findings in PowerPoint "decks" instead of multichapter Word documents.[15]

Susanne Cohen learned these lessons when she brought her anthropological training to the burgeoning field of design research. In her first postacademic job, she helped make better medical devices through participant observation. As she describes it, the job was similar to fieldwork, but without the theory: she now studied people with the express goal of improving products they used in clinics, operating rooms, and even homes.

Susanne continued to build on her experience as she branched into new professional areas. Her work as a principal user experience (UX) researcher at Elsevier required less direct ethnographic observation than she'd done in the past, but she was still called on to aggregate qualitative data and apply her findings to make products more valuable and intuitive to the people who used them. In fact, her chief project in that role brought her closer to her old life than she might have guessed: she served on a team to build and continually improve Elsa, a web-based tool for publishing academic, scientific, and medical books.

Her doctoral training has provided an unexpected benefit, too. Across the roles Susanne has held since leaving academia, she has interacted with people who possess advanced degrees of their own. These individuals have included the doctors, medical specialists, and university professionals who participated in her research, as well as colleagues who also found success outside

15. "Slide deck" or "deck" is nonacademic parlance for a slideshow.

the field they trained for. This point of contact has helped her build rapport faster than she might have done otherwise—and quickly establishes her credentials with audiences that place a high value on expertise.

While Susanne's career is decidedly a break from her academic past, she still sees signs of continuity. In the modern economy, this makes sense. For all that Susanne had to learn new skills and adopt new objectives, the training and habits she acquired from her advanced degree have enabled her to add value to initiatives in academia, medicine, and information technology. Her current company clearly recognizes the benefits she brings to the table: less than two years after she started, they awarded her a promotion.

Conclusion

Most people begin the journey you're embarking on with immense dread about what it might hold. It's essential to confront these fears. For most academics, the single greatest barrier to leaving a "life of the mind" is admitting that you might want to go. Once you recognize this psychological constraint, it becomes easier to imagine and adopt new paradigms of how your work relates to your personal identity and broader goals.

You're not alone in walking the path ahead, and there's even cause to be excited about where it might lead. Don't worry too much if parts of it still seem dark. Confronting dread will give you the strength you need to keep your eyes fixed ahead. And should you ever doubt how you'll see the journey through—or be tempted to retreat back to what's familiar—you can now take comfort in knowing that your current guide and many like him have completed the trip safely before.

Action Items

1. Start a career journal. Your first entry should discuss why you entered academia and how you feel about leaving.
2. Sit down with someone you trust to have a frank discussion about why you want to leave higher education.
3. Do something to celebrate! You're about to start a new chapter.

Career Journal in OneNote
Keep track of
 goals
 skills
 wishes

2

Discern

A few years ago, my wife, Mallory, was a finalist for a tenure-track job at a small Christian college in the rural Midwest. The place looked like a good fit for her on paper, but reality didn't jibe with expectation when she went for her campus visit. She'd been ready for small and religious. In person, it became clear that the school's values and faculty code of conduct were significantly more restrictive than their marketing and job listing had suggested. Some of their policies ran directly counter to her deeply held views—to say nothing of my own. Mallory came home to New Orleans thinking that her obvious discomfort would eliminate her from consideration. In fact, that outcome was what she wanted: she immediately knew the college was a bad fit.

Ten days later the dean called to offer her the job. She did her best to come across as excited without committing to anything. Fortunately, I provided an easy out: the school knew I was also an academic (in the same field, no less), and she insisted that her ability to accept the position would depend in part on me finding work in the area. The dean didn't balk. He offered to fly us up to assess the opportunity together and said they might even make a spousal hire to sweeten the deal.

We hadn't anticipated that last variable. Instantly, the calculation became harder. Mallory soon began questioning how she'd *really* felt on campus: Was she just nervous during the visit? Had the migraine she suffered made her less receptive to the town's charms? Did the school only seem dreary because she visited in January? There were good reasons to think the location might be more livable than she'd initially thought as we looked at it more closely, but the clock on the offer was ticking. We only had one way to know for sure: we booked a flight, packed our bags, and headed north for a three-day weekend.

Despite our cautious optimism that we might be nearing the end of Mallory's academic career search, neither one of us could shake our apprehension. The place really was cold—in both senses of the word—and was much farther from the nearest city than we'd been led to believe. Moreover, when it came time to put real terms around the job they'd mentioned for me, their offer was less a spousal hire than a bait and switch: half-time for one year, "then we'd see."

Everything inside of us said the job wasn't right. Even so, it was hard to trust our gut. Throughout grad school we'd been taught that a tenure-track job was *the* reason you worked so hard, for so long, and at such low wages. And even though we'd always known we'd face the "two-body problem," I wondered whether my anxiety about this particular job derived from concern or jealousy. As our plane home took off, we struggled to balance what we knew was right for us as a family against what we'd come to believe was necessary for success in our careers.

Unsure of what to do, we solicited other academics for advice. A few did their best to frame the issues for us, but they rarely gave us new insights. No surprise there: academics don't talk about turning down tenure-track jobs unless they have a competing offer. When we searched for advice in 2015, the Internet yielded only two results. Both were cases where a position was refused owing to personal or family health. From where we were sitting, that silence seemed to scream a warning: nobody refuses an offer like the one Mallory had before her.[1]

Some colleagues even lobbied Mallory to accept the job—and added a warning. In a year when more than five hundred applicants competed for fewer than thirty-five tenure-track positions, they claimed that turning down an offer could harm her reputation and spell the end of her academic career. This fear had already been lurking in our minds, and although we doubted it was true, we had no positive evidence to contradict it.

Ambition and apprehension seesawed for nearly a week. Eventually, Mallory made a heart-wrenching decision: she gave up a prize she'd been taught to covet for nearly a decade.

Admitting We Have a Problem

As Mallory and I struggled to discern what we wanted in our personal and professional lives, we realized that we'd previously ignored many variables in that equation. That reflex was understandable. Like most academics, we'd been acculturated to think that significant life choices were outside our control.

---

1. As it turns out this isn't actually true. Some academics *do* give up tenure, either to escape an undesirable situation or to pursue a different career. But in many circles that choice is still taboo; consequently, those who remain in higher education after making it tend to be reticent. This dynamic is why things looked so dire from our vantage point: academics were the only people we knew, so the path of turning down a tenure-track job appeared to be untrodden.

You may have figured this out already, but higher ed imposes peculiar demands on the scholars who work within it. Actually, the academic job market is downright weird. Remember that time family members gave you a blank stare as you explained the hiring cycle over a holiday dinner? It wasn't because you're crazy or failed to give a clear account. It's because the restrictions academia places on you are so radically different from what people in other careers experience that they're literally unbelievable.

Even restricting our attention to my opening story, we can note five areas in which higher education hinders your ability to make significant life choices:

- *Location.* Job availability during the five years after you finish your dissertation largely determines where you can live.
- *Acceptance.* Your ability to reject a job can feel like it depends on securing multiple offers in a single year.
- *Timing.* You may apply for permanent jobs only between August and November, and for fixed-term positions between November and April.
- *Relationships.* If you have a partner, they'll have to follow you wherever you're offered a job—or else the two of you can decide to live apart.
- *Track.* Your contract type determines whether you can continue working in a job you're good at; put another way, whether you are hired as an adjunct, visiting, or assistant professor matters more than your teaching quality, scholarly productivity, or community impact.

Buying into these ideas may have made sense when you were rationalizing the demands that higher education would place on you. But these restrictions aren't normal, and accepting them isn't a healthy way to think about your job. Once you've decided to leave academia, it's time to unlearn these attitudes.

For me and Mallory, the job offer described above precipitated that process. The reckoning it entailed was nothing short of profound: she came to see that tenure wasn't the academic track she wanted to take, and I was forced to admit that it might be best to leave the professoriate entirely.

Whatever brought you to the point where you're ready to leave academia, being here presents a unique opportunity to reassess what you want out of life and value in it. It's not just that you *can* answer these questions. You *must*. As you look beyond the ivory tower, retaining old limitations on how you think will hinder you from finding success and happiness.

Moving past the initial dread of considering nonacademic work thus leads you into a period of discernment. In broad terms, this phase of your career transition entails answering three questions that will influence the rest of your journey:

1. What do you want out of life?
2. What do you want out of a career?
3. How can you best align the two?

good questions for career journal!

These issues are about as big as they get, and it's worth saying plainly that I can't just tell you what to think. Your answers will necessarily be personal. I can nevertheless provide a framework that lets you approach these questions mindfully, methodically, and in a way that lets you reliably discern a set of values you can live with.

The tactics I describe in this chapter will help you take a broad view of your life and career—and stop seeing a single job as the sole determiner of your happiness. To reach that objective, you must break down the artificial distinction you're likely used to making between personal and professional success. But discernment of this sort isn't an end unto itself. Its value lies in the power it affords you to make more informed decisions—that is, in the power it affords you to *act*.

Reclaiming Your Life Choices

Upon leaving academia, five areas of your personal and professional life return to your control: location, people, career trajectory, salary, and meaningfulness of your work. Assessing how much each of these areas matters to you is a critical first step as you start out on the path to a new career. Later, these determinations will allow you to prioritize career choices with greater speed and less doubt.

While it's good to give your mind free rein as you practice discernment, remember that these categories can overlap and that privileging one necessarily creates ripples across the others.

A few examples will make these caveats clear. Deciding to live with a spouse who stays in academia may prevent you from choosing where you reside. Likewise, moving to Silicon Valley may open doors in tech, but it also forces you to pursue a lucrative position to cover the high cost of living. Trade-offs are inevitable, but don't let them prevent you from acting. Be mindful about what you choose and why you do so, then commit to a course that aligns most closely with your values.

Let's begin with one of the chief rights you regain by leaving academia: deciding where to live. At a basic level, this choice might entail choosing between city, suburbs, or country. Alternately, you may want to relocate somewhere that has personal significance or presents a specific opportunity. You might even view changing careers as a chance to live in a foreign country—or to repatriate after an extended stint abroad.

Despite the plethora of theoretical options, most people's choices are limited in practical terms. Cost of living may determine whether you can afford to reside in a given area, while those who want to live outside their home country likely need to speak the local language in order to do so. Geography can also limit the specific jobs you're able to pursue. After all, you're most likely to find work at an organization that's close by. Simple numbers can also make your search easier or harder: the more governmental departments, companies, and charities that have offices where you live, the easier it is to find a job. But this general rule isn't absolute: you may be able to find a remote position that allows you to work anywhere with reliable Internet access.

———

2. People are another factor you're now free to consider. Do you want to be closer to siblings or parents? Or maybe farther away? That choice is yours. You're also free to live where you have a cluster of friends. Perhaps that's where you grew up, went to college, or earned your graduate degree, though it could equally be a city where a critical mass of friends managed to find work. *Where* they are doesn't matter. If you place a premium on being close to people you love, align your career search to that priority.

This freedom will be especially exciting for those of you in a relationship. I know what it's like to be "long distance" with a partner—and to worry that a job will make the situation permanent. If you're currently in that position, leaving academia will relieve a significant source of anxiety.

Some of you may have more timely concerns. If the insecurity and demands of academia have prevented you from starting a family, you can now freely ask whether you'd like to consider doing so. A "yes" to this question will create a flurry of secondary considerations: Which areas have the best hospitals or schools? Where are you most likely to find a partner to settle down with? What geographies make it easiest for you to adopt?

———

3. You can also apply discernment to your career trajectory. By this I don't mean *what* you do to earn a living, but rather *how you'd like your career to proceed* as you advance through it. Two brief examples will clarify this distinction.

Let's start with a familiar path. Most academics follow what I'll call an eminence model in their career, building a reputation for excellence in a given area, then working to remain a leader in it. Promotion to higher ranks is common, but doesn't significantly change your day-to-day tasks. Whether an assistant or full professor, you still teach classes, labs, or seminars; conduct research; and present your findings in a variety of forums.

This professional arc is what first drew Chris Papadopoulos to academia. While growing up, he'd seen many family members work in medicine, another field in which specialists advance by continually deepening their expertise. A career in physics thus had the benefit of feeling familiar—and of being easy to explain to relatives back in Greece! It was only when Chris was unable to follow this path that he sought a new way forward: instead of building complex computer models for particle accelerators, he now works as a data scientist for Credit Karma.

Other career paths are nevertheless possible. Michael Zimm wanted to use his PhD in history to earn a deanship, be a provost, or even serve as a college president. He intended to teach and conduct research at each level, but thought his daily tasks would evolve throughout his career. In contrast to the eminence model described above, I term this a leadership model. On this track, you establish yourself in an organization, get to know it intimately, and take on increasing levels of responsibility for its operations as time goes on.

Unlike assessing where to reside or who to live with, discerning an ideal career trajectory is about separating *what* you do from *how* you build your professional reputation. Thinking on this higher level enables you to imagine jobs beyond research and teaching—and may help you realize that the career arc academia offered wasn't ever one you wanted.

This framework nevertheless has limitations. First, the models above represent stock types. Few people ever follow one of them precisely, and there are other models (and metaphors) that may reflect your aspirations better. If you're interested in these alternatives, the Internet provides a wealth of resources. Second, neither of these career options is "correct" in any absolute sense. Ultimately, you'll need to figure out a path that works for your personality and target careers that can take you where you want to go.

———

4. Salary is a fourth area of your career change where discernment is required. People who have found jobs beyond the professoriate emphasize this topic above nearly all others—and also note that it's a subject where academics tend to be squeamish. Career counselors back up this anecdotal point and attest that this attitude is especially pervasive among students of the humanities.

This issue is to my mind one of acculturation. Throughout grad school, we're conditioned to say we're passionate about what we study and told that making money isn't the point of our vocation. Over time, this idea gets ingrained in our psyche, and we come to associate a degree of poverty (or at least the absence of wealth) with the very act of doing our job.

Such convictions can lead you to suffer many indignities you shouldn't tolerate. We all know people who shouldered the expense of moving cross-country for a one-year job or took "remuneration in books" in place of monetary compensation when reviewing a submission for a publisher. These burdens can even become a point of pride as academics try to one-up their peers in showing how dedicated they are to their calling.

The general consensus of those who've left higher education is that life gets much better once you jettison these beliefs and adopt a more pragmatic approach to your career and compensation. Whether you end up deciding that wealth isn't your primary concern or that it's worth pursuing for its own sake, there's no escaping a simple reality: money is the tool our society uses to help people acquire goods and services they want or need. No amount of romanticizing what you do to earn it is going to change this essential fact.

At the same time, embracing an idealism that downplays the value of money is self-defeating, as it allows academic institutions to exploit the very people who care most about them. Steve Jobs was passionate about using technology to transform how humans live, but nobody suggested he should work for free. I would encourage you to start thinking about money the same way. There's no shame in wanting to receive fair compensation for your work—and thus no reason to scoff at the idea of demanding it from your employer.

Your background will necessarily shape your views on this topic. While David Engel was an academic, he aspired to a bohemian life that eschewed financial concerns and privileged a life of the mind. Studying Plato and Aristotle gave him formal language and intellectual cover to defend this position: they dismissed worries about money as déclassé and urged their followers to value truth and reason instead.[2]

Despite these commitments, David spent his years in grad school dining with professors, cultivating a fondness for wine, and coming to appreciate the workmanship of a good wool jacket. Myopia initially prevented him from seeing these contradictions, and it was only years later that he realized why: his upbringing had been remarkably similar to the ancient philosophers he'd studied. Although they were earnest in their conviction that truth mattered above all else, the privilege of their personal situations meant they never *had* to work—and made it easy to profess that money didn't matter.

But a material safety net is worthless in protecting against a psychological fall. After years of equating identity with intellectual commitment, David's pursuit of a new career forced him to seek a new sense of self. In doing so, he had to confront the fact that his old views of himself hadn't mapped onto reality—and that he'd even been guilty of snobbishness. These realizations made leaving academia harder for him than it had to be, especially when he began a new career in a data-entry cubicle at a major bank.

More than a decade later, David is now a managing director at Wells Fargo Advisors, and money stands (somewhat ironically) at the center of his professional life. Despite the challenges that this transformation entailed, the nobler aspects of his old philosophy remain: David still cherishes wisdom, and

2. One of the great ironies of ancient philosophy is that almost every thinker who expressed a disdain for money lived comfortably as a member of the elite.

regularly attends career forums to advise academics on avoiding the pitfalls that tripped him up in his youth.

Kristi Lodge's experience was wholly different. Raised by a single mom, she learned from an early age that it's important to have enough money to pay the bills. She consequently entered her PhD in medieval studies without any emotional connection to the so-called life of the mind: she knew there's only so much you can trade off in terms of money, and that real financial limitations should be avoided.

The personal narrative of "sacrificing yourself for a higher ideal" that marked David's story didn't carry weight with Kristi. Whenever she approached a job offer, she reflexively weighed it against her cost of living and other expenses. This calculation wasn't hard, but it was extremely powerful: knowing the break-even point for her monthly cash flow and how much she wanted to save let her enter negotiations with open eyes—and enabled her to speak on her own behalf from a position of greater strength.

Today, Kristi has struck a balance between financial security and personal integrity that works for her. By day, she's a career advisor for the University of Oregon's Lundquist College of Business, while at night she runs her own company, IncipitCareer, that helps academics find work in other industries.

These stories elucidate the range of attitudes you can take to money as you exit the professoriate. Of course, there are no right answers: you get to choose if your salary isn't important, if it's the only thing that matters, or if it's something between those two extremes. In making this assessment, just be honest about the role you want earning potential to play in your life and prioritize it accordingly.

———

5. The final area of discernment I'll consider is the <u>meaningfulness of your work.</u> As I've already said, many academics view their career as a vocation. With that commitment comes the feeling that what you do matters in a real, existential sense. Whether you're advancing the limits of human knowledge or shaping the next generation of citizens, the stakes seem high—and the work feels worth doing.

It's nevertheless important to ask yourself how much it matters that you pay your bills by laboring for an existential good. Some people are content having "just a job" and find deeper fulfilment in hobbies, family, or charity work. Others are dissatisfied if they don't align their career more closely with their values.

good points of reflection

When considering where you want to stand along that spectrum, be careful not to confuse the tax structure of an organization with the mission that drives its work. Odds are, you will work for one of three classes of employer: <u>business (for-profit)</u>, <u>foundations and charities (nonprofit)</u>, or <u>government (public sector)</u>. While these designations sound like they may provide useful information about the work an entity does (or at least what they prioritize as they go about it), they're not very helpful in practice.

not helpful designations

First, many for-profit companies do significant good in the world. They deliver essential services, improve quality of life, and support charities that are aligned with their corporate mission, their employees' values, or the needs of communities where they operate. Conversely, plenty of nonprofit foundations exist to advance an interest rather than provide direct aid to people who need it. And as I write this manuscript in 2019, governmental programs across the globe are being politicized more than ever, with many of their activities driven by partisan fervor rather than need and consensus.

"Social ventures" complicate this picture further. These organizations aim to address systemic issues plaguing society while operating as a for-profit. Skeptics may assume this model is about capitalizing on misery, but it really can advance the common good. Let me explain. Adopting a for-profit tax structure allows social ventures to attract investors instead of donors. Accessing these larger pools of money can enable a company to fund innovations and scale up solutions more easily than they could as a charity. In short, social ventures can have a bigger impact faster. Making money remains one of their goals, but profit isn't their primary motive.

I know I've been muddying the waters, but I'm working to a clear point: the type of work an organization does depends more on its mission, culture, and values than on its legal structure. In deciding how much you care about your work having an impact on the world, it's *those* attributes you need to consider.

My discussion has thus far assumed you'll work for someone else, but some of you will choose to *found* a business or nonprofit. This path entails its own challenges, but it rewards you with greater control over what you do, how much you work, and who you collaborate with. When it comes to aligning your job with your values, it's hard to beat being the sole determiner of meaning and how to pursue it.

To be honest, I didn't understand these distinctions when I began my career search. I thought nonprofits were good and corporations were bad, and I struggled to imagine holding a position that wasn't at least adjacent to education. I also placed a premium on work that I believed was good in a metaphysical sense—and shuddered at the idea of being a corporate lackey.

Times clearly change. Today, my job is to help a colossal for-profit organization win new business. But contrary to what you might expect, I didn't have to compromise on my values to bridge the gap between my old thinking and my current role. Instead, I had to redefine what I meant by having an impact through my career.

One way I changed my perspective was by reframing the concept of importance. I'd long assumed that my academic work was more complex than any challenge people tried to tackle in the world beyond it, and falsely equated difficulty with significance. Learning about other careers quickly corrected this misconception. In fact, the work undertaken by companies, nonprofits, and governments today is just as thorny and intellectually demanding as the hardest projects I devised in the library. Many are even more so.

It's also hard to overestimate how different work can feel when the stakes are genuinely high. As an academic, I studied a minor Roman poet with a minor global audience. Nobody was made better or worse by my insights: all I did was inflect a "scholarly discussion." On the other hand, the projects I support today shape how companies will do business in the future, potentially impacting thousands or even millions of people. The pressure of getting that work right is energizing—and provides an adrenaline rush that I never experienced as a teacher and scholar.

You may also worry that the people addressing the world's challenges through corporate or governmental avenues are less equipped than those in academia to develop nuanced and equitable solutions. I'll admit that I was long guilty of holding this arrogant view—and I'm happy to report that the people I met while searching for a new career quickly corrected the misconception.

A nonacademic job also allowed me to embrace other parts of my life more fully. My wife and I were able to start a family, and my company gave me sixteen weeks of paid paternity leave during my son's first year of life. That benefit didn't just let me bond with him right after he came home, it allowed me to serve as primary caretaker while Mallory resumed her career and reacclimated to teaching.

The charities I care about have also benefited from my career change. As I noted at the end of the last chapter, work in business has trained me to think strategically and taught me about organizational design and operations. This new knowledge enables me to guide groups like the Nyansa Classical Community more effectively and to connect them to a wider network of donors and supporters. It's always nice to realize that I can afford to offer them more regular financial assistance, too.[3]

———

Throughout this primer on discernment, I've tried to make it clear that the most important outcome is finding a balance of priorities that's comfortable and works for you and your family. I've been happy decoupling my impact on the world from the way I make money to support it. You'll no doubt make different choices. But until you figure out how much meaning you want your work to have—and how you define having a "positive impact"—you won't be able to pursue jobs that adequately align with your values.

---

3. The Nyansa Classical Community is an educational nonprofit that teaches moral imagination and cultural knowledge through its engagement with Greco-Roman, Judeo-Christian, and African American literature. I currently serve on its board.

Discernment beyond a Career Change

Although I've been presenting discernment as structured and direct, it's really a free-form and iterative process—a habit you can and should adopt not just when you step away from academia, but even after you've secured a new career.

David Stevens demonstrates how this works in practice. While a grad student in Princeton's Department of Politics, he was struck by the extent to which scholars were treated as intellectual intermediaries for local populations during policy development. This dynamic initially made sense. Policy institutes form recommendations using reports from experts—and the audiences they advise view academic affiliation as a shorthand for quality or validity. The broader ecosystem thus tends to favor scholarly analysis over direct report.

David found this situation harder to accept as he proceeded through grad school. It was then the early 2000s, and communication technologies were emerging that made it easier than ever to link people across the globe. David quickly saw their potential as an inexpensive way to supplement traditional expertise with unfiltered first-person reporting from people who had lived or were living through the issues he sought to remedy.

History made the continued reliance on a narrow stream of mediated voices all the more frustrating. Western outsiders have a long and bad habit of speaking for locals in regions they colonized, a fact David was keenly aware of as an expert in Africa. Even so, the nature of his research compounded this feeling: David studied the reintegration of ex-combatants after civil wars. Given this subject matter—and the fact that few scholars had real experience of the issue—there seemed little reason *not* to bring more African voices to the table.

Dissatisfaction with this state of affairs contributed to David's decision to leave his doctoral program. Although he recognized that his expertise in African politics could provide an easy off-ramp to consulting—many companies pay people well to help them manage risk in the pursuit of profit—he knew he wouldn't be happy going down that path. Rather, he felt compelled to remain "annoyingly true to his curiosity" and decided to seek new ways to make expertise more accessible.

David's impulse to prioritize impact over money has led him to a life of serial entrepreneurship. After leaving Princeton, he undertook contract work related to African politics and policy, then began volunteering with a think tank in New York—a city he'd long been eager to return to. These decisions satisfied his intellectual drive and desire to choose where he lived, albeit at the cost of long hours and low pay.

Eventually, though, David's efforts afforded him a substantive opportunity: the World Policy Institute (WPI) hired him as their director of strategy. In this role, he was able to advance a broader vision of how to engage the public in policy discussions—and later to reimagine how to pursue his work in that organization most effectively. In 2019, WPI dissolved, selling its assets to a new company that invited David to serve as founding director and acting CEO. In that capacity, he is building a social venture on the legacy of WPI and exploring innovative ways to raise awareness of and interest in complex issues of public policy.

David's career has thus advanced by aligning his work ever more closely to his personal values and convictions. Discernment initially led him from academia to a nonprofit. From there, it inspired him to help found a new corporate entity that is committed to the public good. This path hasn't always been easy, but David's attempts to divine what's right for him each step of the way have allowed him to look back without regrets.

Practical Exercises in Discernment

If you're still not sure where to start with discerning a path through the fog, a few exercises can help you ease into the process.

One option is to keep a journal of the activities you tend to enjoy and avoid in your professional and personal lives. This simple, low-effort strategy can help you identify patterns in your interests over time, especially if you still have a few years before grad school or a contract runs out. *journal*

When tracking my own interests, I found myself despairing at the thought that I might teach the same course on Roman history every semester for the rest of my career. That epiphany let me see just how much I value variety in my work—and indicated that I would chafe against any job that was highly repetitive. Before I'd begun seeking careers outside the professoriate, I already knew I wouldn't be happy teaching high school.

If your time frame for leaving academia is compressed, you can enlist a friend to debrief you on your experiences in higher education. Engaging in such a conversation will help you pinpoint the activities, dynamics, and challenges that drew you to this work in the first place, as well as the obstacles and difficulties that drove you away. Later, you can use your notes from this discussion to narrow down the jobs you want to pursue.

While the specific questions you ask yourself may vary based on your discipline, here are a few to get you started:

1. What first got you excited about your academic field?
2. What do you enjoy most and least in the work you do?   *journal*
3. What benefits did you expect an academic life would afford you?
4. When do friends and family say you're at your happiest?

The goal of these activities is to shake you loose from your assumptions about what makes you happy in academia—and to help you recognize the aspects of life and work that you're most eager to prioritize. As always, there are no right answers, only insight that allows you to act with greater certainty.

From Living to Learn to Learning to Live

What follows is a discussion of how Mallory and I practiced discernment in the face of the tenure-track offer described at the start of this chapter. It's meant to be illustrative rather than prescriptive, explaining how we grappled with competing variables to arrive at a decision that was right for *us*, not what *you* should do if put in the same situation. My goal in describing this process is merely to model how you can balance what you want or need from your life and career.

In confronting a possible move to the Midwest, we quickly realized that *location* mattered to us greatly. Although we'd entered the academic market believing we had to go wherever jobs took us, New Orleans had knocked us off balance. It wasn't just that Mardi Gras was in full swing and that the town we were asked to move to was cold and quiet. We'd come to love this city's history, architecture, and vibrant food and music. These luxuries were accessible and affordable to us—and made life appreciably better than in other places we'd resided. Looking north, the picture was bleak. The best restaurant near the college in question was famous for its mashed potatoes.

People were a big part of the equation, too. Although Mallory and I didn't know anyone when we arrived in New Orleans, we quickly became friends with our neighbors and joined an array of social clubs. For two newlyweds in their late 20s, life was a dream: we had monthly cookouts, Mallory started playing roller derby, and I was elected president of the local homebrew club.[4] In less than two years, we'd become true members of the community—even though we'd spent that entire time warning friends that work would eventually force us to leave.

By contrast, the community we were being asked to join was notoriously closed. We weren't opposed to making new friends in a new location, but also didn't see many openings for us to thrive. Neither of us knew a soul within three hours, and more than one person volunteered without prompting that the primary way you plugged into the social scene there was through a church—ideally of the local Protestant variety. It was also rumored that the school's "powers that be" tracked attendance at services. That last claim may have been exaggerated, but it was still worrisome for two sometimes-regular, more often less-dutiful-than-we'd-like Catholics.

We also worried about our families being, at a minimum, two flights or a full day's drive away. Distance already prevented them from visiting New Orleans as often as we wanted, and we knew they'd be less likely to travel to a snowier, more remote destination.

Salary was also a problem. The school offered Mallory a compensation package around the (academic) market average, which meant I would need to find work if we wanted to afford a house, children, and the inevitable cost of trips to visit family in the Northeast. Options were limited. The spousal position they mentioned to pique our interest was only short-term, and the other nearby colleges were uniformly small and equally unlikely to have the budget for an extra Latin professor.

---

4. My non-American readers may be scratching their heads here. A cookout is a barbecue, roller derby is a full-contact women's sport played on roller skates, and homebrew is the hobby of making obscene quantities of beer at home, both for personal consumption and for foisting on skeptical friends and family.

Although at this point I still believed my future was in academia, I even looked at jobs in other sectors. None looked promising. Even if they had, the situation would have been untenable. The nearest city was an hour's drive from where we'd live. In good conditions. In a region that gets snow five months a year. Maintaining two homes was also out of the question. Apart from the cost, we had no interest in living apart after five years of long distance in grad school.

Facing unemployment worried me for another reason, too. I've always known that I love intellectual challenges and like to think I'm at my best when laboring to solve them. Given this disposition, it seemed all but certain that my psychological health would suffer without the stimulation of a career. Neither Mallory nor I was eager to test that hypothesis. We knew that the strain of prolonged unhappiness wouldn't only harm my well-being—it could also threaten our relationship.

Concerns about salary thus overlapped with what accepting the job would mean for us as a *family*. Once the "tenure clock" is ticking, every academic knows there's a mad dash to write and publish until you've passed review. But that six-year stretch of time can be awfully long when you're also thinking about a *biological* clock. Although Mallory was well within child-bearing age, she was hesitant to delay having kids for the better part of a decade.[5]

Even if we had found a way to make that situation work for her professionally, the thought of raising children in a community whose values went so much against our own was chilling. I worried about what kind of friends a son or daughter might

5. Nandini Pandey's 2019 article "Not Bringing Home a Baby" is a beautiful and crushing account of her attempts to have a child while pursuing an academic career: https://eidolon.pub/not-bringing-home-a-baby-b6dc15a3701.

grow up with, and what sorts of assumptions they would make about the world as a result. I also recoiled at the thought that my wife and I might appear to approve of the school's moral leanings or be complicit in supporting a system that perpetuated them.

Thinking through what life would look like in this position also allowed Mallory to learn something important about her *career trajectory*. Once she was on the tenure clock, she would have to publish articles and write a monograph in her narrow area of expertise: Greek biographies of the historical period after Alexander the Great. For all that she loves reading those texts, she had doubts about the value of investing so much time on formal research that has an extremely limited audience.

As she thought about this issue further, she came to see that the renewable "professor of practice" position she held at Tulane aligned much more closely with her personal and professional aspirations. This teaching role carries no obligation to publish and allows her to focus on outreach and pedagogical innovation—activities that have a real and immediate impact on the communities where she lives and works. Ironically, these are also activities that many university presidents trumpet, but that tenure committees view as "nice to have" rather than as a basis for advancement.

Our conversations also allowed us to see that tenure was the *only* benefit that made the position in question superior to Mallory's current job: her teaching load would have been the same, the salary was only negligibly higher, and she would have had fewer resources available for travel and research. That last concern was especially worrisome. She knew that failing to publish at least a few articles (and ideally a book) within her first six years would lead to "nonadvancement"—which is to say, she'd be fired.

Stopping to think in pragmatic terms also helped us recognize that the position was less secure than it seemed. The
college relied almost entirely on tuition to fund its operations,
even though demographic trends in the area suggested that
revenue stream would shrink as Mallory's career progressed.
What's a professor to do if their school shutters when they're
fifty and they haven't published an article in fifteen years? As
a friend likes to say: all faculty are contingent, even if most
don't realize it.

In short, the position Mallory was offered is what I've come
to call a "tenure-trap job." These are professorships at remote
schools whose teaching load is so heavy, labs or library so ill-
equipped, and funding in such short supply that you can't conduct research on the scale needed to make a lateral move to a
better position at another college. It's not that they're *necessarily* bad jobs. The students may be smart, you may be excited
to live in the area, or there may be something about the school
that's an especially good fit for you as a person. But for anyone
who accepts such positions with the intention of moving on to
bigger opportunities, they're decidedly a quagmire. And the
only way not to get stuck in a quagmire is to avoid walking into
it in the first place.

This period of discernment also had an unintended consequence. As we sought to justify Mallory's rejection of a job that
was an exceptionally bad fit for our family, we became aware
of all the trade-offs in an academic career that we'd silently
accepted during grad school. Shining a light into these shadowy
recesses made us realize that tenure-track positions weren't
likely to give either of us what we wanted: Mallory's renewable position could satisfy her professional goals, and we were
confident New Orleans would keep delivering the quality of
life we valued.

My work was the one remaining variable in this calculation. Knowing that I couldn't remain an academic without abandoning the woman or city I loved, the choice was easy to discern: I had to find a new career.

Conclusion

Discernment is much more than an exercise in navel-gazing: it serves a practical end. By stopping to reassess your broader goals, you put distance between yourself and the details of your academic work. This distance, in turn, affords you the perspective to think beyond *what* you do and to identify *what makes you happy* about doing it.

Achieving this wisdom is an essential step on your path away from academia, because only when you know what you want out of *life* can you figure out what's truly viable for you as a *career*.

Action Items

1. Clear your schedule and take a day for yourself. At the end of it, reflect on the activities or relationships that drew you in when you were free from standing commitments. Log these preferences in your career journal.
2. Remind yourself of the life goals you had in high school or college. Jot them down in your career journal, then question whether they still hold—or whether you've simply been putting them *on hold*.
3. Ask where you'd live if you could pick anywhere in the world. The answer will clue you in to your driving values (environment, proximity to family, pace of life, cultural ethos, etc.).

3

Discover

When I finally realized an academic career wasn't in the cards, ignorance of how to proceed drove me to a desperate plan: I went through my Facebook friends name by name seeking *anyone* who had earned a doctorate but wasn't a professor. Pickings were slim. In fact, the only person who fit the bill was Dan Porterfield. He'd been a vice president at Georgetown when I was an undergraduate there, but by the time in question served as president of Franklin & Marshall College.

My respect for college hierarchies—and my self-consciousness about imposing on a superior's time—made me hesitate to contact him. Even so, I felt there was no one else I could turn to. Early one Saturday, I wrote Dan a note and slowly built the courage to press "send."

If I'm being honest, I didn't expect a reply. I hadn't spoken with Dan in a decade and suspected he was far busier than when I'd seen him last. While these doubts swirled, it dawned on me that he might even have an aide manage his online presence.

Seventy-six minutes is all it took for Dan to write back. His note was brief, but he sent it himself—and extended an offer to chat by phone.

I spent the days leading up to our call reminding myself of Dan's career path. As I understood it, he earned his PhD, secured tenure, then moved to administrative roles by way of university service. A comment to this effect early in our chat drove the discussion in a new direction. He quickly disabused me of my assumptions.

During grad school, Dan hadn't focused single-mindedly on academia at all. He'd been a Rhodes Scholar and a Mellon Fellow, sure, but he also worked with the charity he founded as an undergraduate and served as a speechwriter for an administrator at the City University of New York. That record took him far, *far* beyond the library: in 1993, he became a senior aide to Donna Shalala, who was then secretary of the Department of Health and Human Services under President Clinton.

Dan served in that role for four years, and only then turned his attention back to academia. For a time, he threw himself into teaching, research, and all the other activities that can advance your case for being hired on the tenure track. But an old friend had other ideas. He knew of an open job in strategic development at Georgetown and thought Dan was a good match. It helped that he was in a position to know: the person in question was Leo J. O'Donovan—at the time Georgetown's president.

Dan was interested in the opportunity, but the role wasn't exactly what he had in mind for the next stage of his career. He decided to hedge. By way of a counteroffer, he asked that he be appointed to the English Department on top of his administrative job. Being a member of the faculty would let him keep teaching and give him a position to fall back on if strategic development didn't work out.

Dan never had to activate that contingency plan. He soon found that he enjoyed his new work and quickly progressed to more senior positions, culminating in the offer to serve as president of Franklin & Marshall.

But our discussion didn't end with me being corrected on these biographical points. Dan also gave me tactical advice to facilitate a career change: seek any and every opportunity to learn new skills, make sure I got paid for extra work I did at my college, and don't bother getting another degree to appear more qualified. Additional schooling wasn't going to give me what my situation now required: practical experience.

As I reflected on that call over the subsequent days, I realized that I'd long based my understanding of Dan's career on how I wanted my own to proceed. That version of him was essentially a mirage. This realization was illuminating—and furnished three valuable lessons.

1 First was the extent to which baseless assumptions had informed my views of the industry I was training to work in. At the time, it was inconceivable to me that academia valued anything beyond scholarship, and I believed leaders were selected because of their work in that area. While Dan *was* celebrated for his research—his dissertation won the Irving Howe Prize— the more remarkable turns in his career occurred because he built practical skills, engaged with issues of the day, and cultivated relationships with people who were in strong positions to champion his cause.

2 Second was how Dan found greater success by forging his own professional path than he could have done through a traditional academic career. I may have been unusual, but I entered grad school wanting to support a college's strategic initiatives through service in its administration. I assumed—wrongly—that the only path to that life was through the professoriate. Dan's story made it clear that holding jobs at his level took a willingness to break away from what was familiar.

As I reflected on those insights, it also dawned on me that I'd confused seriousness for single-mindedness throughout and after grad school. I was a decent scholar and—I still believe—an excellent teacher. But my pursuit of excellence in those fields was so total that I'd ignored other essential aspects of my life. I had few hobbies, did nothing to help the less fortunate, and spent the little free time I had trying to shut my brain off. At the time, I called these behaviors the marks of a dedicated scholar. In hindsight, they made me one-dimensional—and a total bore.

Ultimately, these choices about how to spend my time resulted from another assumption: that being a serious scholar would lead to a successful career. I'd always been promised in grad school that "good people got good jobs." I'd taken this belief to heart, convinced that I would end up on the right side of the statistical divide if I could commit myself ever more fully to my discipline.

As I later learned from my work on contingent faculty issues, academic jobs don't always go to the best candidates. Any position could have multiple applicants who look like an ideal fit, but only one of them can receive—and accept—an offer. Likewise, factors such as who your advisors are, how well you wrote your application materials, and what jobs are "hot" relative to your area of expertise interact in such a way that success in the process can look like luck. The truth is that many good people don't get offers—or get offers that aren't good for them.

In the meantime, my miscalculation had cost me. By focusing on classics to the exclusion of everything else, I missed opportunities to develop new skills, meet new people, and conduct more interesting and multifaceted work. Dan's story showed me that being one-dimensional isn't a reliable way to succeed, even within the academy.

3   Third was that Dan modeled a type of servant leadership that I wished to emulate. He didn't get anything from spending part of his evening on the phone with me—and I suspect he would have rather caught up with his wife or children. But more than anyone else I know, Dan believes in the value of mentoring generations behind him and helping others thrive. Being on the receiving end of this kindness rekindled my desire to be a "person for others," that is, someone who uses the short time we get in this life to improve the world, rather than retreating into selfishness and self-interest.

Dan's career also proves that selflessness and success aren't mutually exclusive. After making Franklin & Marshall a national leader in the recruitment and support of first-generation college students, he got a chance to have an even broader impact: Dan now serves as president of the Aspen Institute, a nonpartisan forum that brings leading thinkers from academia, industry, and government together to solve the world's most complex problems.

Opening Your Eyes

My conversation with Dan Porterfield filled me with hope and inspired me to think that, with a little gumption, I could find an on-ramp to a new career within a college setting. Thoughts swirled about working on Tulane's accreditation renewal efforts, supporting undergraduate admissions, or finding work in the president's office. After all, one university president had thought I was worth his time, so why wouldn't another?

In hindsight, this belief was almost as naïve as my recently shattered views of how Dan's career had progressed. I was entering a world that I knew nothing about and still had much to learn before success would rise to meet the confidence I tried to exude.

Even so, being naïve isn't always bad. It brings high expectations and feelings of strength, two sensations that will be refreshing to those of you who feel constrained by academia. When you experience this change in outlook, you'll know you're entering a new phase in your career transition.

Whereas discernment lets you untangle the web of limitations academia imposed on your personal and professional life, *discovery* provides a chance to learn what careers are available and open to you. Throughout this process, you must ask yourself:

1. What work could you do?
2. What work do you *want* to do?   *journal*
3. What are the most obvious gaps in your experience?

This stage is ultimately about opening your eyes to what's possible. By the time I finally did so, I'd spent more than a decade cultivating expertise in a tiny sliver of human knowledge. If you're reading this book, you're presumably in the same situation. The problem for people like us is that the deep focus and dedication that let us succeed in academia are precisely the opposite of what's required to thrive outside it. If you want to find a new career, you have to break old habits, try new things, and shape yourself into the kind of person others trust to improve the organizations they serve.

Beholding the Wider World of Work

Each day, *billions* of people support themselves by working outside academia. This fact may appear so obvious as not to warrant mention, but few of us ever take the time to consider what those individuals do or how they perform their jobs.

Consequently, we tend not to know *how much we don't know* about the wider professional world.

Most of us, of course, have at least some familiarity with jobs other than the ones we've trained to do. If you lived on campus as an undergrad, you likely have friends who are lawyers, doctors, or consultants. My own parents are accountants. The trouble is that a little knowledge is dangerous: having a small degree of familiarity with a small number of jobs can lead you to overlook two glaring blind spots.

First is an issue of breadth. Even if I'd mapped out everyone I knew and every job they'd done when I began my career transition, I would have only seen a small fraction of the careers that exist in the world. That limitation is unavoidable, of course, but it's one we don't often admit. To put the matter bluntly, knowing four professions besides my own was awfully close to knowing nothing.

Second is an issue of depth. For all that I knew about my friends and family, I'd never taken the time to talk with them at any length about the details of their work. I had a vague idea of what it meant to practice law or prepare a tax return, but little knowledge of what that work was *really* like or what skills were required to do it. This failure was of my own making—and ultimately rooted in the same self-absorption I'd indulged in during my years in grad school.

While your understanding of the world beyond academia may not be as deficient as mine was, I'm willing to bet it's not as precise as you'd like. For now, I'll recommend a simple remedy: keep your mind as open as possible to the work you might be able to do and the kind of career path you'd be willing to take. Assume you can do *anything*. There will be plenty of time later to figure out whether a career is practicable for someone with your strengths, skills, and experience.

I know that heeding this advice isn't easy. It took me extensive practice to quiet the voice in my mind that insisted, "You're not qualified for that job," or "You'd hate that kind of work." But the truth is that I had no good basis for making those judgments when I was first contemplating a departure from academia. To move past the fear that you can't succeed in a new career, you have to put everything back on the table.

That said, you'll be able to dismiss some career options faster than others. I'm terrified of needles, which makes jobs in acupuncture, tattoo artistry, and medicine bad bets. Even so, I forced myself to entertain those thoughts for a (very) brief period of time. This exercise opened my eyes to work in sectors that I wouldn't otherwise have considered—especially the plentiful nonmedical jobs in New Orleans's local hospitals.

As you begin the process of discovery, it's also important to set limits on how long you can afford to explore new possibilities. I know: this advice sounds ironic after telling you to cast a wide net. But setting constraints on time is different than limiting scope. It's easy to get distracted by the joy of learning and put off the harder task of preparing to enter a new professional world. Believe me: I know all about "productive" procrastination! It's an enticing trap, but one you should be careful to avoid.

If you're a grad student, at the start of a multiyear contract, or a tenure-line professor, allow yourself six to nine months to explore new careers. The amount of information that's about to *6 - 9 months* hit you can feel like an avalanche. You'll be able to dig out more effectively if you adopt a slow, deliberate approach.

Many of you, though, will be under pressure to find a new job as quickly as possible. Let your individual circumstances dictate how much time to give discovery: first, calculate how long you have between now and your last paycheck, then reserve a third of that period for exploring new careers. At a minimum, this effort deserves a few days or weeks. Pausing to survey the path ahead allows you to advance with a measured step and will give you greater confidence when you start applying for jobs. While engaged in discovery, you can also begin the activities described in the next two chapters.[1]

Informational Interviews: A Primer

Some of you may be wondering how you can learn about jobs when you don't even know what they are—or that they exist. Simply put, you ask. By meeting as many people as possible and inquiring about their careers, you'll quickly get a sense of what jobs are available, what they're like on a day-to-day basis, and what long-term prospects they offer.

These conversations are most commonly called "informational interviews." They are *not* an opportunity to ask for a job. Rather, they're a way to learn how somebody got where they are so you can gauge whether their work is something you'd be interested in doing.

For academics used to working alone, informational interviews may sound intimidating. Many of us are introverts by nature, and grad school often acculturates us to avoid imposing on other people's time—especially if those people outrank us. I used to hem and haw for half an hour before asking my *dissertation advisor* for a fifteen-minute meeting. Coming from that mindset, it initially seemed odd (actually, it seemed rude) to ask somebody for thirty to sixty minutes just to chat about work.

---

1. Consider starting with the section on "Making Time for New Activities" in the "Develop" chapter.

But the rest of the world isn't like academia. Most people relish an opportunity to break up the tedium of routine work, to meet new people, and to talk about themselves. Consequently, informational interviews aren't just normal: they're usually welcome.

Consider yourself lucky if you're already comfortable striking up a conversation with strangers. This phase of your transition should be fun and easy: just start finding people who interest you and ask for a meeting.

Those of you who are hesitant about this activity can start by searching the Internet for guides on how to conduct a *journalistic* interview. These manuals will teach you how to prepare for a discussion, manage its flow, and react to unexpected silence—as well as how to synthesize your notes and distill them after the fact. Although an investigative conversation aims at a slightly different end than an informational interview, the skills that enable success are the same in each context.

As you ease into this unfamiliar type of interaction, consider conducting your first informational interviews with people you know. Sit down with a parent, another relative, or a close friend and discuss what they *really* do for work. It might seem stilted to speak to these people like strangers, but that awkwardness wears off once you begin a genuine back-and-forth. Your existing relationship will also help the conversation along: not only will you find your interlocutor easier to speak with, but their knowledge of your situation will allow them to frame their comments more precisely.

The point of these initial discussions is *practice*. One half of that effort is getting comfortable with a new mode of discourse, which the conversation will itself allow. The other is being coached on ways to improve. That goal requires you to end your sessions by asking your partner to assess what you did well or awkwardly from the vantage point of someone in their line of work. Prompt them to critique your introduction, questions, eye contact, responses, clothing—anything that stands out. Nobody has to hit each of these topics (it may be awkward, for example, to ask your mother about your clothing), but you should cover all of them at least once before you start interviewing people you don't know well.

Next, incorporate any feedback you receive into your self-presentation. People outside higher education behave differently from those within it and sometimes view our professional tics as arrogant or off-putting. During my time in academia, for instance, I adhered rigidly to grammatical rules and constantly alluded to obscure parallels from my discipline. These behaviors were harmless in the world of classics, where everyone was in on the game, but they weren't cute to nonacademics. They made me stand out and—worse than that—made people uncomfortable. That latter outcome wasn't one I could afford. Consequently, I worked to adopt a new manner of speaking that was better suited to my new audience.

A cynic might describe my behavior as that of a chameleon, but my aim was to meet my audience where they were—and to make our conversation more comfortable and enjoyable *for them*. I would advise you to do the same as you identify personal tics that others interpret as overly weird or academic. Ultimately, informational interviews are about asking strangers for help, and people are more likely to provide that help when you come across as somebody they'd like to spend more time with.

Once you've completed a few practice interviews, it's time to extend discovery to people you don't know. To identify new subjects, start with sources close at hand. Maybe you'll know a colleague who left your program before finishing their degree, read about an administrator on your college's website, or see an article about someone using their PhD in an unexpected industry. It doesn't matter who they are or what they do: just identify people who've taken interesting paths that you'd like to learn more about.

Next, find contact information for these individuals and ask them for an informational interview. The best way to reach out is email or LinkedIn. When you send your note, keep it brief. State who you are, how you found their name, and why *3 sentences* you're writing—namely, because you're changing careers and want to learn about their professional development. Anything more than three sentences is too long. Although that might sound curt or even rude, the opposite is actually true: providing extraneous details steals time the person hasn't offered you.

The following example should provide a good starting point:

Karen,
My name is Chris Caterine, and I'm currently seeking a new career after ten years in academia. Your history caught my eye while I was scanning LinkedIn, and I'd love to learn more about how you got where you are today. If you're open to meeting for coffee, please let me know your availability and I can set up a meeting.

Not enough detail for me

Thanks,
Chris

If you're still apprehensive about reaching out to strangers, remember that you don't have much to lose in soliciting them for advice. The worst-case scenario is that they say "no" or don't reply. In my experience, these reactions were rare: about 80 percent of the people I asked to interview agreed to speak.

A few ground rules will help you keep these meetings on track. First, it's best to interview your subjects in person—at least when you're starting out. Doing so is for your benefit more than theirs: while you're new at conducting these discussions, you want to have as many cues as possible about how they're going. Intonation, body language, and other nonverbal signals can tell you when somebody is open to further questions or is eager to move on. The better you get at leading a conversation the other person enjoys, the more likely they'll be to keep in contact and help you in the future.

COVID !

Second, remember that you're asking somebody for their time. It's therefore prudent—to say nothing of decent and courteous—to thank them in a substantive way. Picking up the tab for coffee or a drink at happy hour is an easy option. I'm constantly amazed at how generous people can be with their working hours for an outing that costs me less than ten dollars. Of course, even that amount of money will strain some grad stipends and adjunct wages. If so, budget what you can, knowing that the potential return on this investment is considerable—and that the salary you'll earn in a new career will more than make you whole. Planning to pay the bill will also give you an excuse to meet in a neutral location, which may put you at ease if you're nervous about visiting someone's office.

The procedure for an informational interview is simple: introduce yourself, explain what you want from the meeting, and ask an open-ended question about how your interlocutor got to the current point in their career. After that, listen intently and follow up when you hear a detail of their story that interests or confuses you. I found it was helpful to take notes, but I always asked before doing so.

To determine whether you're well suited to a given career, devise questions that are likely to uncover pertinent

information. I make two inquiries of this kind in every informational interview: (1) What are the skills you wish you had before
you started in your current role? and (2) What have people
gone on to do after holding your position? These questions let
me assess the immediate gap between my current capabilities
and what's required to do a job and allow me to identify how
many doors a specific career is likely to open.

I discovered the benefit of this approach during an interview
with an admissions officer at Tulane in the summer of 2015. At
the time, I was still committed to working at a university, and
this career path seemed particularly viable. In fact, I could claim
to have practical experience: I've interviewed undergraduate
applicants to Georgetown University since earning my BA there
in 2007. When I asked my interlocutor what her colleagues had
done *after* being admissions officers, however, her answer was
disheartening. Most used their tuition waiver to earn an MBA,
then moved to another sector. Those who were committed to
pursuing careers in admissions worked in lower-level jobs until
someone above them retired—or they found a better position
at another college.

Although I walked away from that interview disappointed
with the outcome, on further reflection I realized that it simplified my search. I knew I didn't want to earn another degree—
and I had absolutely no interest in pursuing a *second* career
where people got excited for a job to become available through
an unexpected death or arrest. Eventually, I realized that the
half hour I'd spent in the interview was well worth the time: it
had taught me that college admissions wasn't a field I wanted
to pursue, and that I wouldn't have to give it another minute
of thought.

As this story demonstrates, informational interviews have
the potential to teach you an incredible amount about your

career options even when they don't go to plan. You might learn about a new area you'd like to consider for work, but you can just as easily become aware that you *don't* want to do something you assumed would be a natural fit. They're also hard to mess up. Since the other person in an informational interview does most of the talking, there's little risk that you'll bore them or cause offense. The only place to be careful is in making sure the conversation doesn't drag: if your interlocutor loses interest or seems to be winding down the conversation, take the initiative to thank them for their time and wrap up gracefully—even if it's only been ten minutes.

At the end of these meetings, it's helpful to ask whether your interviewee knows anyone else you can speak with. This *snowball sampling* old journalism trick expands your reach organically and lets you get a note of introduction instead of having to contact new people out of the blue. This question is also a useful proxy for gauging how willing they are to assist you in the future: the more people they mention as contacts—or the faster they follow up after your meeting—the more attentive you should be to maintaining the relationship.

It's also good to send a follow-up note within two days of the interview. Doing so isn't just a chance to say "thank you" again: it allows you to remind your contact of who you are and show that you value the time they gave you. A handwritten letter isn't necessary. A simple email expressing gratitude and summarizing which parts of their story you found most helpful will suffice. This note can also be a good opportunity to request introductions to other contacts one last time.

The number of meetings you're able to conduct will depend on where you live and how much time you can commit to the practice, but I'd recommend you average no fewer than one per week. Maintaining this pace will help you quiet any jitters and overcome the initial learning curve as quickly as possible.

But it's not enough to meet people on a regular basis: it's also important to build these new relationships. I try to reach back out to people I interview roughly six to eight weeks after our first meeting. That message reports concrete ways I've taken their advice and (implicitly) reminds them that I'm still seeking work. Any response is a good sign that the person is interested in getting the update, and an enthusiastic one may indicate that they're open to meeting again. Seizing these opportunities lets you deepen your new relationships without coming across as needy—and can even lead to genuine friendships.

I found that my calendar was the easiest way to maintain correspondence at the frequency I desired. Whenever I sent a thank-you note after an interview, I would also set a reminder to follow up with the contact six weeks later. That said, you may be drawn to other techniques. If you use your inbox as a to-do list, for example, you can employ a tool like Boomerang to refresh old messages at fixed intervals and remind you that they require attention. Alternatively, you can maintain a spreadsheet of interview contacts and add columns to schedule or track each new exchange.

Throughout this section, I've shown how informational interviews can teach you about new careers. They're also useful for learning about dynamics in a particular region or industry. Although this latter information may not seem valuable to you just yet, it can make a critical difference for timing your departure from academia. I'd thus advise you to track it from the start of discovery.

Chela White-Ramsey demonstrates how you can use this information effectively when the time eventually comes. Since she knew Austin, Texas, had a burgeoning tech scene and plentiful jobs for young professionals, she began conducting informational interviews there even before she'd completed her dissertation on human resource leadership at Louisiana State University. Those discussions taught her that rapid software development and implementations in the region had sparked a growing need for learning and training—precisely the activities that had drawn her to academia.

Although Chela saw a rising wave in Austin that she could ride for the first part of a postacademic career, she also had another semester of fellowship that could support her as she wrote her dissertation. These competing opportunities made it hard for her to know the best way to proceed. Ultimately, the risk of inaction proved more motivating. After informing her advisors that she would forgo her fellowship, Chela quickly found a job as a technical writer for Travis County, which houses Austin. She completed her doctorate while working there the following year.

Checking Other Sources

Informational interviews provide a wealth of information about new careers, but the work doesn't end when the discussion is over. After you get home, review your notes and consider whether your interviewee's job appealed to you. Specific topics to consider include your general impression of their profession and career path, as well as the specific elements of their job that drew you in or gave you pause. If you struggle to get your thoughts into words, try discussing these topics with a partner or friend. A debrief of this sort will help you clarify your lessons from the encounter and provide an outside perspective on elements of it that excite you most. More often than not, my wife spotted patterns in my interests before I did.

Next, consult independent sources on jobs that excite you. National job boards like Indeed.com, Monster.com, or equivalent sites in your country can provide a sense of what skills you need to qualify for a given position. You'll know you've struck upon a true requirement when you recognize a pattern across similar jobs at multiple companies. If the skill or knowledge set in question intrigues you, ask about it in future informational interviews or start building it right away (for more on the latter topic, see the "Develop" chapter). Inversely, if you have no interest in doing what a job requires, you'll know you can move on to other possibilities.

You can also read books or blogs that treat the problems different sectors are trying to overcome. Many of these resources are published by or with the consent of companies that have a vested interest in advancing their views of a problem—and thus reflect how *they* (as much as the authors) wish to frame new solutions in those areas. If you're worried that a job outside academia won't be intellectually stimulating, these discussions can reveal whether you'd be satisfied with the challenges a given job might ask you to address. Don't worry if you lack knowledge about a given topic: writing of this sort normally adopts a colloquial tone that is accessible to nonexperts.[2]

Search engines can also allow you to uncover more information about careers or companies that interest you. Try pairing keywords you've learned through contacts with skills that they described having. Often, you'll find websites or articles related to specific jobs—or even uncover positions you didn't know about that are better suited to your strengths.

2. These documents are often termed "white papers," "eminence," or "thought leadership." Examples of such publications include *Deloitte Insights, Jane's Defence Weekly, McKinsey Quarterly*, and the *World Policy Journal*.

Information from the above resources is useful, but its full potential becomes apparent when you plug it into LinkedIn. This tool is essential in today's labor market. Putting millions of curricula vitae at your fingertips, it lets you see both the roles that led people to their current work and the skills they possess that enable them to do it. Best of all, it can sort results by geographic area. This feature is critical for someone undertaking discovery, as it allows you to identify people in your community with a job or skill that interests you. In other words, LinkedIn offers a virtually limitless supply of possible targets for an informational interview.

Using these digital resources is how I met Andrew Foley, the person who first made me consider business more seriously. I found his name on the site of a local consulting firm, where his bio mentioned that he'd previously earned a master's degree in music at Johns Hopkins. Later, he decided that path wasn't for him, left academia, and won a fellowship with Venture for America—an entrepreneurial equivalent of Teach for America.

Although I was still apprehensive about trying to "cold contact" new leads for an informational interview, Andrew's story was too close to my own to let the opportunity pass. I wrote a brief note and emailed the company's "Contact" address to ask him for a meeting. I didn't have to wait long for my boldness to pay off. Andrew replied later that day. In less than a week, we were sitting down for drinks. And within two months, he'd convinced his former boss to interview me for an open job.

The meeting Andrew got me didn't turn into an offer, but it started a chain reaction of informational interviews with an entirely new circle of people in New Orleans. I spoke with local consultants, a school system operations director, and an independent marketing agent, among others. In fact, as Andrew's contacts passed me to their own friends and colleagues, I was able to schedule at least one informational interview or phone call every week for nearly a year. The excitement of these developments had a profound impact: never again did I hesitate to contact someone I didn't know.

Self-Awareness through Discovery

Discovery isn't just a linear process: it's also iterative. As you build knowledge about jobs through interviews and research, you should also reflect on your discussions and work to refine your conversational form. If meetings don't go as planned, identify why and assess whether different choices could have produced a better outcome. When they go right, ask yourself whether the positive result came from natural chemistry or from tactful decisions you made in leading the discussion. Drawing lessons from each conversation will allow you to improve continually—and to build a deeper knowledge of diverse career paths.

Eventually, repetition and improvement in discovery come together to produce the distinct feeling of *momentum*. All your practice meeting new people, reaching out to strangers, and researching careers quite different from your academic field will forge once-foreign behaviors into second nature. Before you know it, you'll be able to fire off an email for an informational interview in two minutes and prepare for the conversation itself in under ten. If you're anything like me, you'll even start to have fun meeting new people—and feel lazy if you go too long without learning about a new profession.

You'll also come to see patterns in your career interests that can help you target opportunities more precisely. That moment of clarity came for me when I realized that the parts of academia I had always loved the most—and the work I wanted to do in the future—focused on helping organizations convey their strengths and vision. Formulating this idea allowed me to narrow my job search to positions in communications strategy, an area of marketing that translates missions and differentiated skills into discrete messages intended for discrete audiences.

This epiphany reduced the number of job *titles* I was considering, but expanded the number of sectors where I thought I could work. After all, every organization has to communicate its vision to the outside world, and most employ people specifically to do so. Informational interviews allowed me to see this fact more clearly—and to recognize that a career in communications strategy fit my personality and background.

While you'll necessarily have different interests and speak to different people than I did, your outcome should be the same: if you build discovery into your career change, you'll learn what you need to know about the jobs you could do and the ones you're excited to seek.

Networking 101

So far I've treated informational interviews as a means of discovery, and to my mind they're the most efficient tool for that job. But they also build a *network* of people who can help you in your career search.

If you're anything like me, you may have feelings about this type of relationship. I long considered networking perverse— an attempt to *use* people for personal gain when they should have been *befriended* for joy and companionship. This cynical interpretation assumed that people who "networked" only made nice with contacts to get a job, and that they did so to the detriment of those (like myself) who respected a regular hiring process.

If this dynamic were true, I would still be a skeptic. But after throwing myself into networking for over five years, I now see it as an indispensable practice that can be equally beneficial and enjoyable to both parties.

My change of heart was sparked by the realization that very few people are in a position to hire you at the precise moment you meet them. Consequently, *networking isn't about getting a job*—at least not directly. It's instead about increasing how many people you know within a company, field, or geographic area. The more people you know, and the more actively you maintain your relationships with them, the more attuned you'll be to the dynamics and concerns that impact them. Likewise, the better they'll know what kind of position you're suited to.

"If that description is correct," some of you may be wondering, "how does networking differ from informational interviews?" I'd point to two major distinctions. First, networking entails openly cultivating someone as an advocate in your career search. That individual may be a person you met through an informational interview, but could just as easily be a friend, an academic colleague, or even a relative. Second, networking involves more sustained relationships. This latter attribute is often what prevents it from becoming utilitarian: most people will only help you in your career search if you maintain a good rapport, and few networkers have the patience and skill to fake that dynamic convincingly over months or years.

To understand how networking can lead to job opportunities, it helps to take a high-level view from the vantage point of *all* parties, rather than just the person seeking work.

At its heart, networking is an efficient way to connect Person A who has skills (in this case, you) with Person C who needs them (that is, an employer). The efficiency that makes this type of relationship so valuable lies in Person B—the individual who knows both parties and realizes they can help one another. The goal of networking isn't to meet the Person C who can hire you: it's to cultivate lots and lots of Person Bs who can connect you to opportunities you're unaware of.

Put another way, networking exponentially increases the reach you have within a market by using your advocates (or "contacts") as proxies to help you find work. I advise you to start this process with informational interviews because they can do double duty: you learn about a new career *and* add a new Person B to your network. Maintaining the discipline to keep those discussions informational—that is, *not asking for a job* until you know the person better—also makes it easier to convince them to introduce you to their contacts. Nobody expends political capital asking an acquaintance to talk with a random academic. And in any case, everyone you meet in that context will know you're looking for work.

A more advanced networking technique is to serve as an intermediary yourself. When you hear that a contact is looking for a new job or recruiting for an open role in their company, introduce them to people who might be able to help. Assistance of this sort isn't just nice: it shows that you want them to succeed and will leverage your own relationships to make that happen. At that point you're *really* paying them back for the support they've given you—and building good karma in the process.

Although you might struggle to imagine connecting people in this way right now, conducting one or two informational interviews a week will build your network quickly. Before you know it, you'll likely find yourself in a position to be someone else's Person B.

Explaining Your Career Change

During informational interviews, it's important to keep the focus on the other person. After all, you can't learn anything unless you get them talking. But most of the people you meet will be polite. They won't want to seem like they're hogging the floor and will look for chances to turn the conversation back on you. In any interview, you may face questions about your background, why you're leaving academia, and what kind of jobs you're interested in. Whenever this happens, remember that it isn't just a sign of good manners: knowing your interests and what you'd be good at lets your interlocutor be more precise in connecting you to other people in their network.

Consequently, you always need to be ready to tell your story. This advice may seem obvious and easy to act on, but talking about yourself can be harder than you'd expect when your audience is a stranger from outside academia and you're planning to ask them for a favor. I still remember the first time someone asked me why I was trying to change careers. My response was abysmal:

Well, my contract at Tulane is terminal, which means they have to let me go at the end of this year even if the department wants to keep me. And while everyone said the job market was bad when I finished my dissertation, the last two years have been way worse in my area of expertise. I got one interview for a tenure-track job in 2014, but came up empty the last two cycles.

My wife and I also want to have kids at some point, and a professor's salary isn't enough to raise a family—especially if we both follow jobs and have to live apart from one another.

But we did long distance for five years in grad school, and we're not willing to do it again.

Anyway, I know I'm really good at what I do. I have to imagine there's a way to put my skills to use outside of a classroom—I just don't know what it is yet.

Let's break down what makes this narrative so bad. First, there's nothing positive in my answer. I start with a negative, end with a negative, and wedge lots of negatives in the middle. The response is also focused entirely on me. I allude to forces that acted on me in one way or another, but only consider how I suffered as a result.

Just because this portrayal reflects how I felt at the time doesn't mean it was right to say out loud. For all that self-indulgent complaints may feel therapeutic, they don't give other people a meaningful way to join your conversation. What could the woman sitting across from me ever have said to make me feel better—let alone done to alleviate the burdens that were weighing on me? She didn't work in academia and only knew what I'd told her about that environment.

Making this situation worse was the fact that she'd come to the table to network. At this point in time, I was new to informational interviews and insufficiently practiced at thinking about what my *interlocutor* might hope to get from our discussion. If I hadn't been, I might have thought to reply in a way that demonstrated forward-looking interests or even positive skills that I could bring to a new work environment. Instead, she got an arrogant assertion that I was smart.

It was obvious to me even in the moment that this version of my career change hadn't landed well. And while it was too late to change my response on that occasion, I developed a far simpler response that I brought to subsequent interviews:

When I started grad school in 2007, an academic career looked "medium risk, medium reward." Since the recession, it's become "high risk, low reward." Once I realized that new dynamic, it became clear I had to make a change.

I suspect you'll agree this is better, but let's assess why. First, my new response tells a story. There's a setup, a crisis, and at least a move towards resolution. I also limit my focus to details that let me convey *how I responded* to external forces rather than *how I felt* as they acted upon me. These elements make the story easier to understand—and provide accessible jumping-off points for more meaningful exchange.

Second, this account frames my career change in terms that make sense outside of academia. In place of the horrors of the job market and the burdens of contingent life, I focus on risk and reward. This concept is part of the vernacular, and in business it's a natural way to view the world. Likewise, my revised story passes the smell test: everyone knows the economy was bad in 2008, and few will be surprised that academics suffered, too. This last element is to my mind one of the story's greatest strengths: it invites other people to connect their experience of the Great Recession to mine.

Third, I get to the point quickly. There's no fumbling with an overdetermined choice or psychoanalyzing of decisions that other people made. While this version of events may not reflect the "whole truth" of my situation, nobody ever said it had to. In fact, I've learned from informational interviews—as well as my current job—that most people expect simple answers to simple questions. Those who want more nuance or detail will ask for it.

My simpler, more engaging account ultimately stems from a small change in perspective: instead of conveying what changing careers felt like *to me*, I highlight the details of it that will resonate *with my audience*. This framing allows me to answer the question asked without getting bogged down in extraneous, inaccessible information. And brevity has an added benefit, too. By returning control of the conversation to my interlocutor as quickly as possible, I empower them to guide the discussion wherever they're most interested. Put another way, I keep the focus on them even when they've asked a question about me.

As you refine an "elevator pitch" that reflects your needs and personality, keep in mind that each change of audience requires a change of message. This dictum is a basic lesson of ancient rhetoric—something I knew well as a student of the classics. Even so, I initially found it hard to apply because it felt like lying to tell my story in different ways depending on who I met. Overcoming this apprehension took another lesson from my days as an academic: hard facts can't be changed, but arranging them into a story always entails choices about what to include or leave out. All I'm advising you to do is to make those choices with others in mind.

When adopting this approach, it's helpful to work backwards from the views or knowledge that your audience is likely to have. Try to infer their frame of reference by researching them on LinkedIn (at a minimum) before you sit down to chat. If they come from a background in business, talk in terms of opportunities, threats, and profit. If you're interviewing the director of a charity, relate what you've done to the greater good, social headwinds, and the need for change. Don't stretch your framing beyond what's credible or use metaphors that make you uncomfortable, of course. But nor should you balk at speaking in a way that's consciously designed to resonate with the person across the table. At the end of the day, you're trying to win them over. Achieving that end starts with speaking their language.

Sticking with It

Meeting people, maintaining relationships, and reshaping your story time after time is genuinely hard. After a few weeks or months, these activities can become a slog. One day, your stomach may turn at the thought of conducting another interview as you want nothing more than to take a break.

I would strongly advise you to fight this urge.

During the early months of 2017, I had run myself ragged conducting informational interviews, working ten hours a week for a friend's business, writing a blog, volunteering with two charities, and applying for jobs—in addition to teaching three courses. Even at the time, I knew the pace was unsustainable.

Panic struck when Mike Zimm emailed to say he'd never copied an acquaintance on an introductory email four weeks before. He assured me I'd like the person in question, and I knew the call could be beneficial to my career. Even so, I found myself inventing reasons to turn it down. I recalled that nothing came of an application I sent to the contact's company months before, even though a college friend had referred me for the job. Moreover, I was deep into the interview process for a position in New Orleans and felt good about my odds of getting an offer, albeit ambivalent about the role. Even at the time I recognized these excuses for what they were: attempts to convince myself that the informational interview was a waste of effort because I was desperate for a break.

Despite that reluctance, I forced myself to take the call. Guilt was a driving factor. Mike had gone out of his way to make the introduction and followed up when he saw that it got lost in transmission. Even if he never found out that I cancelled, it would have been disrespectful of the time and effort he put in on my behalf. I was also aware by then that people have limited political capital to expend on introducing you to their contacts. If I blew off the meeting in question, it would have been harder for Mike to ask this person to help other academics in the future. That last realization proved impossible to shake: I wanted it to be okay to act in my supposed self-interest, but couldn't bear the thought of harming others who were also struggling to change careers.

I can't overstate how glad I am that I did the right thing. Mike's contact soon put me in touch with another former academic at his company—in fact, the person who had hired him. That call went well, and before I knew it, I was being considered for the job I currently hold.

Talking to Nonacademics

There's another side of talking to nonacademics that we haven't addressed yet. In fact, it's one of the most important lessons you have to learn. When you're pitching your experience to people in other areas, you have to ~~become a lot more concise~~ | ~~be more concise~~ | be concise.

Professionals in other sectors commonly fault academics for talking around issues and taking forever to get to the point. I'm sorry to report that they're right. After four months in my current job, I attended my academic discipline's annual conference. While there, I was struck by how rarely speakers could state the significance of their argument and how often questions focused on minor issues instead of substance. I even got bored at a panel on my area of expertise.

On reflection, I realized that there's a good reason why dialogue differs so much between academia and the world beyond. The point of research institutions is to give very smart people nearly limitless time to understand issues from every angle. This investment is what makes research valuable: scholars' mastery of their content enables them to make discoveries that wouldn't otherwise be possible. The flip side of this coin is that academic culture requires you to show all the work you've done to justify claiming that your contribution is "new." That display of learning can drown out the main point.

Other fields don't operate on the same schedule or with the same assumptions. There's never enough time to dig into every issue requiring a decision, and the people in charge of complex organizations count on those below them to separate the signal from the noise. In these environments, extraneous information isn't just a waste of time—it's a distraction from other critical responsibilities. Consequently, while you're still expected to understand your area of responsibility in minute detail, you're largely judged on your ability to distill and prioritize that information efficiently.

Shifting from an academic to a nonacademic mode takes time, and building the habits of thought and speech required to do so is a secondary goal of discovery. As you learn about new careers, you should simultaneously work to convey information in ways that meet the expectations of your new audiences.

Fortunately, there's a simple way to diagnose whether you've taken too long to get to the point—at least in writing. If the first time you state your conclusion is in the final line of a document, you've missed the mark. Instead, *start* with the key information you want your audience to take away, then provide the fewest number of details needed to justify that position.

In business, the standard acronym for this procedure is **BLoT**: "Bottom Line on Top." Doing it consistently is how you avoid the reply **tl;dr**: "too long; didn't read."

I've benefited immensely from learning to get to the point— and would offer two reasons why you should do the same. First, writing this way is effective. Like it or not, most people don't read every word on a page; in fact, they usually stop after about three lines. Fronting critical information increases the likelihood that people with less patience will get your message, while those who are interested in details can still read on to get a fuller picture. You don't cut anybody out by conveying information in this order, you just accommodate a group that longer responses will alienate. Second, this mode of writing is efficient. Starting with your conclusion shows the reader where subsequent information is headed, helping you—and them—focus on the details that advance your larger point.

Putting the bottom line on top is an easy way to correct a leading culprit of verbal bloat. With practice you'll get better at prioritizing key details—and even start to do so when speaking, too. Slowly but surely, you'll start to sound like your future colleagues instead of an academic.

Applying the Lessons of Discovery

I end this chapter with another story. Although it comes from later in my career search, I tell it in "Discovery" for two reasons. First, it shows how informational interviews will help you present yourself more confidently when it's time to seek work in earnest. Second, it teaches an important lesson about how exploring new careers can provide the perspective you need to select a *good* one when a job offer finally comes.

It was the last semester of my visiting contract and I was beginning to panic. I'd been meeting with lots of people, taking their advice, and doing whatever I could to build my résumé. Everyone assured me I would find work soon, but New Orleans is a tough market for young professionals. I hadn't interviewed for a job since the summer, and we were getting into crunch time. Soon I'd be unemployed.

As my faith in the value of my degree began to evaporate, so did my pride. I started applying for every job I could find. Legal practice assistant? "Take my résumé." Office support for a shipping logistics company? "I'll never be late for work—I live close by." Beer promoter? "I've been homebrewing for four years. Sounds like a good fit." Even if I wasn't thrilled with all of these opportunities, I figured I was seeking a new career and would have to start at the bottom. And some of these jobs really were rock bottom. Think beer promoter sounds fun? It's a nice name for the guy who pours samples in the grocery store.

In the sea of positions I was applying for, one caught my eye. A national life insurance company had a marketing position available, but they didn't want anything via email: you had to call directly. That request was unusual, and I figured it couldn't hurt to see what it was about. I called and left a message with my name and number.

The recruiter got back to me fast, and after screening my résumé, he invited me in for an interview. I was ecstatic! This was the first time in four months someone was considering me for a job.

Given the line of work and the way I'd been screened on the phone, I figured the position was in sales. So I prepared the way I always did for an informational interview: I reviewed my experience and found anecdotes that might interest my target audience. My pitch was brief. I claimed that sales was a good fit for a teacher—especially one who made boring topics seem exciting—and that I had experience navigating New Orleans's diverse populations. That last claim was perhaps a stretch, but I could at least claim that I got on well with my students at Tulane and the old libertarians in my homebrew club, as well as the academics I worked with in various capacities.

I apparently struck the right tone. The first interview went really well, and the two men running the process quickly invited me back for a second meeting, then a third and a fourth. They were forthright all the way through: they confirmed that the job was in life insurance sales and said that the work, while not for everyone, could provide a nice life for those it suited. Their four-interview sequence was in fact designed to give both sides adequate time to gauge whether the opportunity was a good fit.

There were other positive signs, too. The person recruiting me had spent a few years teaching high school until—like me—the chance of a higher income led him to a new career. He'd even been promoted within a year or two of joining the company. When that detail piqued my interest, he suggested I might be able to follow the same trajectory.

This job interview was also the first one that felt natural to me. We bantered back and forth, moved smoothly from small talk to serious concerns, and generally struck up a positive rapport. In my other job interviews, I'd been far more nervous— and my emotional state made me come across as uncertain when success depended on confidence. This time, however, I didn't feel out of my league. I spoke to the two people across from me as equals, and they seemed to be eating up everything I had to say.

But let's not forget: these were life insurance salesmen. They're experts at making whoever they're meeting feel at ease—and they'll consider anybody with a pulse.

This dynamic became clear as the process continued. My first warning was that they delayed discussing salary and compensation until very late. When it finally came up, they spent an hour insisting on the simplicity of the structure they used to reward high performers, a system that included multiple com-mission rates in several tiers that were based on the number of sales you made in a given month and the number of years since you'd initially sold a policy that was then being renewed, as well as lump-sum payments that kicked in when you met certain monthly sales thresholds. At the end, I made the mistake of trying to summarize: "So there isn't a salary, per se. The job is 100 percent commission." They quickly rebuffed this assertion: there *was* a base salary each month—it just kicked in after you'd made a certain number of sales. I'm no accountant, but even I could see that calculation didn't tally.

Friends and family in financial product sales also warned me against going into life insurance. One person who's known me forever insisted I was too smart for that line of business: not only did he think it was a waste of my talents, but he was certain I'd get bored.

The same person was able to explain that the hiring strat-egy for entry-level jobs in insurance sales is dodgy at best, and even borders on predatory. Here's how it works: As soon as you're hired, they immediately have you sell to family, friends, acquaintances, and anybody else you know well enough to guilt into buying a policy. This initial bump in sales lets you make a decent wage—which is the bait. A few months in, however, most people run out of contacts. At that point, your commis-sion falls off precipitously unless you can sniff out strangers and convert them into sales. The majority of new hires can't, so the majority of new hires quit. Here comes the switch. After you leave, you don't keep earning commission on the policies you sold to friends and family; instead, it goes to the person who recruited you.

I'd also conducted enough informational interviews by this point to know that I should ask about career path. Insurance offered a limited number of options: you sell policies or manage salesmen. The only alternative would have been a lateral move into another type of sales. There's nothing wrong with those options if they're appealing to you, but two aspects of my personality made me certain they were a bad fit in the long term: I'm not great at asking for a sales meeting, and I'm even worse at closing.

The most obvious indication I'd been cajoled came when the person recruiting me tipped his hand. During my final interview, he extended a formal offer and said he'd call after the weekend to see if I would accept. Silence followed. In truth, I wasn't overly upset: I was apprehensive about the job and figured they had sensed it. Being cut loose would save me the difficulty of having to say no.

The phone rang three weeks later. My recruiter was at the other end, asking if I wanted the job. I politely said I had to pass—but gave him the benefit of explaining my rationale. The biggest problem was the lack of a base salary. To my mind, promising a stable income is how companies display good faith in your ability to do the job they require. At thirty-one years old, I was unwilling to assume all the risk in an arrangement that was supposed to benefit both parties.

When he heard this, the recruiter offered a reply that will stick with me forever: "We talked about how the job isn't 100 percent commission the last time you were in. Did you forget that conversation, or did you just not understand it?"

Well, then. I could see in that moment how he really viewed me, and I knew quite well that my apprehension was well placed. So even though I didn't have any other offers, I thanked him for his time and got off the phone. I was nervous, to be sure, but by then I'd regained the confidence I needed to move forward. After all, if surviving four interviews hadn't raised my sense of self-worth, rejecting someone who insulted me decidedly had.

In any case, the world beyond academia moves quickly. Just two months later, my current employer offered me the job I hold today.

Conclusion

Discovery is a critical stage of your career transition that allows you to learn about the world beyond academia. As discussed throughout this chapter, informational interviews are an efficient tool for undertaking that effort. They'll help you get familiar with diverse careers, let you figure out where there are gaps in your résumé, and set you up to be more confident when you finally pitch yourself to the wider world.

Even so, a successful career transition depends on more than knowing lots of jobs and lots of people: you also need to communicate your strengths and value to the people who can hire you. That undertaking requires a new set of skills—and cultivating them marks the next phase in your professional transformation.

Action Items

1. Find someone from your discipline who's left academia and arrange your first informational interview.
2. Practice writing shorter emails that start with the main point and only provide information that's strictly necessary.
3. Come up with a twenty-second version of why you're leaving academia that frames your departure in positive terms.

4

Decipher

It was the early fall of 2016, and a networking contact managed to get me a job interview with a local consultancy. I read up on the company, practiced telling stories I thought would resonate, and picked out clothing that seemed businesslike without being too formal. I knew the job was a stretch for me, but was confident I could make a good impression. I walked in with a good feeling that my search for a new career was over.

Confidence got me again. I lost control of the conversation less than two minutes into the interview and never regained it. Every time I tried to prove my commitment to doing something new, the CEO peppered me with questions about the type of work—*academic* work—he thought I wanted to do: reading in the library, working alone, laboring without a deadline. No tack I tried could steer me back to safety. Despite commenting on my interesting background and apparent intelligence, he couldn't see how my skills related to his business. I didn't even get the standard line that he'd let me know about the job: he told me I was a bad fit before I left.

Three months later, the same company listed another position. Again the CEO made time to meet me, and again he couldn't see me as anything but an academic. He professed optimism that we'd get a chance to work together eventually, but after two swings of the bat I wasn't sure. He clearly wasn't buying what I was selling.

These experiences forced me to reconsider my approach. For all that I felt ready to leave higher education, that desire clearly wasn't enough. Something in my self-presentation still screamed "academic"—and was a giant red flag that employers couldn't ignore.

Departing the interview, I did the only thing I could: I thanked the CEO for his time and promised myself I would never again be unprepared to convey the relevance and value of my academic experience. The challenge, of course, was figuring out how to do it.

Making Your Degree Relevant

Many employers will be intrigued by your advanced degree, but they're often skeptical of how you'll perform on the job. The fourth phase of your career transition is about deciphering your academic skills and translating them for a nonacademic audience. Once again, this stage will invite you to answer a set of questions:

1. Why should nonacademics care about your academic experience?
2. How can your academic experience add value to an organization?
3. What's the best way to frame your past work for your new audience?

This work essentially continues the efforts you began in discovery. By shifting your focus from yourself to others and describing your talents in terms they value, you can turn your advanced degree from a weight around your neck into a platform to stand on.

The "Overqualification" Trap

Getting a job is about marketing yourself. To succeed, you need to present a coherent and compelling vision of who you are, what you bring to the table, and how you're different from other people seeking employment.

The biggest challenge you're likely to face when interviewing for jobs is the perception that you're overqualified for entry-level positions, but underqualified for more senior listings. This double-edged sword threatens most academics as they depart higher education. Evading it requires knowledge and agility: once you understand why it's so pervasive and where it strikes, you can more easily dance around it.

Graduate school trains academics to become what people in other sectors call subject matter experts (SMEs)—individuals who have deep knowledge in a specialized area. SMEs commonly advise companies or project teams on issues that require added care or that go beyond the knowledge that novices can acquire as they do their jobs. For example, a software company designing a finance system for a global bank needs to digitize the bank's internal processes in a way that enforces regulatory requirements from all the geographies where the bank operates. Since the software developers aren't experts in banking laws, they call on SMEs to help them write code that complies with legal restrictions.

If you're coming out of school with a doctorate, most people will see you as an expert in your given subject. The challenge you face is that nobody outside the academy can monetize knowledge of Roman poetry after Vergil or constructions of gender in eighteenth-century French novels. Even scientists aren't safe on this count: although your skills are nominally applicable in industry jobs, many still face hiring bias because of the excessive specialization that graduate school requires.[1]

Trying to convince nonacademics to value *what* you study is probably a losing battle. To return to my example above, a software company won't hire an SME in global banking regulations to put her hands on the keyboard and write code. Even if she can do the job, she's unlikely to be the best person for it—at least from the vantage point of a hiring manager. To argue otherwise seems patently unreasonable.

One way to escape this reductive line of thinking is to convince people that you're *not* an SME. I'll discuss the mechanics of translating your academic experience in greater detail below, but for now a simple dictum will suffice: emphasize *how* you study rather than *what* you study.

Focusing on methodology is an easy way to accomplish this end. Every academic field approaches problems in distinct ways—and as someone with an advanced degree, you're highly skilled in using the tools of your discipline to understand, synthesize, and report raw information.[2] Highlighting the statisti-

1. Adam Ruben, "When Ph.D. Stands for Problematic Hiring Detriment," *Science*, January 23, 2019: https://www.sciencemag.org/careers/2019/01/when-phd-stands-problematic-hiring-detriment.

2. Isaiah Hankel, "Why Employers Prefer PhD Job Candidates," *LinkedIn Pulse*, November 12, 2018: https://www.linkedin.com/pulse/why-phds-misunderstood-feared-isaiah-hankel-ph-d-/.

cal theories you apply to historical data or the strategies you use to test scientific hypotheses will be more intelligible (and often more interesting) to nonexperts than the details of what you analyzed.

You can also talk about activities that surround your work in higher education. You've likely managed projects, organized conferences, or guided committees—all of which involve some level of working against deadlines and allocating work effectively. Academics commonly take these skills for granted because they're "table stakes" for people in the professoriate. Failing to mention them in other contexts is a mistake. These talents are valuable, but potential employers won't know you possess them unless you say so.

In a similar vein, you almost certainly possess an array of "soft skills" from years navigating a world where teens, scholars, and administrators are each convinced their interests should be your top priority.[3] While you might not flag these attributes first when you present yourself to nonacademics, it's important to convey how experienced you are at working with people who rank below, equal to, and above you across the many professional contexts that you've occupied.

Some people are naturally gifted at generalizing their academic experience and conveying their strengths with passion and conviction. Michael Zimm, for example, was able to walk into an office, ask for the CEO, and talk himself into a job. This approach is admittedly unusual—and takes a character of special force. Michael's success depended on his ability to convince his new boss that he brought the company's growing

3. Katina Rogers, "Humanities Unbound: Supporting Careers and Scholarship beyond the Tenure Track," *Digital Humanities Quarterly* 15.1 (2015): http://www.digitalhumanities.org/dhq/vol/9/1/000198/000198.html.

team a unique perspective that would help them address problems in ways that differed from their competitors. His encyclopedic knowledge of history and ability to read the room quickly cemented the decision: although the CEO didn't know precisely what Michael would do for the company, he had no reservations about extending an offer.

Other people seek more familiar paths when trying to broaden the appeal of their academic experience. Today, numerous professional societies, businesses, and social enterprises fund "bridge fellowships" to help academics transition to work in other sectors. One benefit of these programs is that the application process is nearly identical to what's required in academia. Another is that selection committees often include former academics who can meet you halfway in your explanation of how you might apply your current skills in a new context.

Positions such as these often look like a perfect way to exit academia, but there's a catch: they're often as competitive as tenure-track jobs—or even more so. Since applicants to these fellowships compete against people from every other field with bad academic job prospects (which is to say, most of them), it's likely *harder* for you to stand out from that crowd than it would be for a tenure-track job.

I had a mixed experience with these opportunities. None of my applications ever led to an interview, but each one advanced my discovery of potential careers and helped me discern which of my experiences were relevant to organizations that did interesting work in my region. I would urge you to adopt a similar outlook. If a fellowship looks like a perfect fit for your background, interests, and personality, go ahead and apply. But don't expend too much effort forcing yourself into molds you don't fit just because the format of the application is familiar.

The opportunity cost is high, and the likelihood of success is exceptionally low.

A more reliable path to translating your academic experience for new audiences is to build an effective résumé. Since this document differs from the curriculum vitae (CV) you're used to, it's helpful to summarize the distinctions between them before explaining how to translate the one into the other.[4]

A CV lists your professional qualifications and accomplishments. Its structure is fairly rigid: education, work experience, publications. While you probably tailor your CV when applying to specific jobs—for example, by changing the order of your research and teaching sections—its components are largely stable. Cover letters consequently play an important role in academic applications. They allow you to call out your addressee by name and flag CV details that are particularly relevant to the opportunity in question.

A résumé is by definition more selective. It's a persuasive document that explains why you're right for a job by highlighting relevant skills and accomplishments. Today, it's often submitted by itself or—in the case of email submissions—with a brief, one- to two-paragraph note. This difference is significant. Since you rarely get to walk your audience through your résumé, the document itself needs to guide your reader to the information that's mostly likely to convince them to speak to you at greater length.

This chapter offers a generic approach to structuring résumés that should work for many sectors. Still, some caution is required. Before you use the model I propose for particular

---

4. While there are countless resources available on fashioning a résumé, chapter 4 of Basalla and Debelius (2015), *So What Are You Going to Do with That,* is especially good.

jobs, read advice specific to the industries you're targeting—and find real résumés from those fields to guide your self-presentation. Different sectors have different expectations, and it's critical that you give your audience the information *they* need to hear to consider you for a position. This research shouldn't take much effort. Use LinkedIn to survey how others cast their professional persona, then reach out to contacts you've met through networking to get feedback on successive résumé drafts.

How to Write a Résumé

Start with your name. Make it large and place it in the top left of the page, where most English readers will look first. Immediately below it, provide a short description of yourself that uses nontechnical terms to state the value you bring to the organization you're applying to. The best summaries are economical—as brief as half a line, and never more than three.

This opening needs to grab your reader's attention. Be punchy. Focus on the big picture instead of writing long sentences that enumerate relevant attributes. It's better, for example, to describe yourself as "Helping organizations deliver projects on time" than to say, "As a visiting assistant professor, Chris has worked on short notice to teach, design courses, build schedules, and conduct research."

Bullet "keyword" skills beneath the summary or in a narrow column on the right side of the page. This format draws the eye and is easier to read. Focus on attributes or knowledge sets that are most relevant for the role you're applying for, using keywords from the job listing to guide your order. If you're unable to divine what matters to the organization that's hiring, list your skills from strongest and most differentiated to weakest and most generic (i.e., "published author" before "basic knowledge of Microsoft Office suite").

A few examples will clarify how to put this generic advice into practice. In the pages that follow, I'll provide text of actual résumés from former academics and analyze their most effective elements. Let's put my own summary on the chopping block first:

> Chris develops clear and compelling messages that help organizations present their strengths and vision more effectively. By day he's a communications strategist and writer for a global consulting firm; by night he advises academics on how they can transition to a new career. He previously spent a decade in higher education as an advocate for contingent faculty and a professor of Roman history and literature. Ask him about:
>
> - Strategic messaging
> - Persuasive writing
> - Proposal development
> - Networking

In writing this blurb, I use simple, jargon-free language to highlight the value I bring to the organizations I support. I begin with my ability to convey big-picture ideas to a wider audience, placing myself in the domain of sales and marketing. My second sentence defines my experience more precisely as a communications strategist, writer, and career coach. Its parallel structure ("by day . . . by night . . .") conveys that I can thrive equally in a corporate environment and in one-on-one discussions with private clients. Lastly, I present my academic background in a way that prioritizes service work over my area of expertise. Doing so keeps the reader's attention on activities that are intelligible to them (advocacy) rather than on subject matter that isn't (Roman literature). As a result, I come across as a generalist rather than an SME.

The bullets that follow the summary let those who are only skimming the page process key facts about me—and check off any requirements they might be scoring my résumé against. Structuring my overview in this way has an added benefit: I can expand or contract the bullets for different audiences. While the version printed here emphasizes my work in pursuit management, my personal website says more about my activities as a career coach.

My biggest criticism of the blurb above is that it's too long. Even though I've held it to three sentences, it stretches beyond four lines. The semicolon is also less than ideal. Since this punctuation mark is rare outside academic writing, it may slow readers down, especially those who are unsure of what constitutes proper usage. In hindsight, I would probably embrace a shorter tagline and hit on the other concepts in a skills list or my work history.

Liz Segran achieved brevity by dispensing with a summary entirely. She distilled her experience into four bullets that provided a matter-of-fact account of why she'd make a good journalist:

Profile

- Expert in South and Southeast Asian culture, history, politics and women's issues
- Effective writer and public speaker
- Diverse professional experience; works well in teams and in leadership positions
- Lived and worked in France, Belgium, Singapore, Indonesia, India, UK and US

This list is short and to the point. It sets forth the knowledge areas, skill sets, and experience that Liz possesses, but doesn't stretch the truth about her background. Although its form borders on blunt, it's impossible to deny that it was effective: this introduction is how Liz began the résumé that helped her get her first nonacademic job.

Comparing that text from 2011 with the biography Liz currently features on her website is illustrative. Although the difference in genre means you can't use what follows as a model for your résumé's *form*, you can imitate its more effective *framing* of her academic experience:

> Elizabeth Segran is senior staff writer at Fast Company, whose work has appeared in a range of publications including *The Atlantic, Foreign Policy, Foreign Affairs, The Nation, The New Republic, The Chronicle of Higher Education,* and *Salon.* Her book, *The River Speaks,* was published in 2012 by Penguin Books.
>
> She received her Ph.D. from the University of California, Berkeley in the field of South and Southeast Asian Studies with a Designated Emphasis in Women, Gender and Sexuality. She is an expert on India, having devoted a decade to studying its history, literature, culture and gender dynamics.
>
> She is a global nomad who grew up in Brussels, Paris, Singapore, Jakarta and London before moving to New York to attend Columbia University. She currently lives in Cambridge, MA with her books, her husband and her baby girl.

This account of Liz's past is effective without being direct. As it flows from current work to personal background, it provides an implicit argument for why she's an effective writer and commentator.

Liz grabs her reader's attention in the first paragraph with a litany of respected outlets that have published her work. The key strategy here is *demonstrating value*. If someone perusing her website reads nothing else, they'll know that Liz is a successful author and journalist. Her professional accomplishments speak for themselves. While this approach may not be feasible until you have nonacademic experience, you should still begin your résumé by stating the value you can bring to the organizations you want to work for.

In the second paragraph, Liz states her academic experience without overselling its relevance to her current work. This balance is crucial for someone in your position. If you want to appear credible, you need to suggest the type of work you *could* do without presuming to know everything about it. Liz achieves this end by highlighting how she spent a decade analyzing the intersection of cultural elements (history, literature, etc.) in the context of India. That skill is essential for a journalist—though Liz never comes out and says so directly.

The third paragraph paints a vivid picture of a life spent moving among diverse cultures and geographies—then pivots to describe the more common experiences of college and motherhood. Liz comes across as interesting but relatable, the sort of person you'd want to end up next to at a cocktail party. Taken together, it's easy to feel like you already know her, even though she's used fewer than 150 words to give that impression.

Don't worry about achieving perfection when you write your own summary. There's no "right" way to make it arresting or engaging—and you'll change how you present yourself over time. Instead, try to adhere to the expectations of the industries you're targeting and avoid coming across as a subject matter expert. If you succeed even moderately in these areas, you'll increase the likelihood that a hiring manager will consider your application more seriously.

Once your opening is complete, it's time to list your relevant work experience. Start with your most recent jobs first, then work backwards. Under each one, put two or three bullets that highlight your achievements in the role. Include only positions that tell an employer something valuable and unique about how you think and work, or what you can do. List any teaching assistantships you held in this section, rather than with your education: doing so will prevent readers from thinking you only *took* classes while in grad school.

As always, remember to put your successes in terms that resonate with your target audience. Under my academic positions, I no longer write that I taught three courses per semester. That statement may be true, but it reinforces the common assumption that professors only work nine hours a week. Instead, I've taken to boasting that I delivered $500,000 in education services annually. Even after more than two years working outside academia, I still feel peculiar framing my experience in this way. Doing so nevertheless makes my past work relatable to my colleagues in business—especially since the number is big enough to sound important.[5]

Those of you who've held multiple visiting assistant professorships (VAPs) may need to make your positions look

---

5. To find this number for yourself, divide your college's annual tuition rate, excluding room and board, by the number of courses students take in a year, then multiply by the number of students you teach.

sufficiently different from one another to keep your reader's interest. Be creative and use the selective nature of résumés to your advantage: no one will be the wiser if you spread six accomplishments from each job across multiple entries—or if you do so in a way that suggests your accolades got more impressive with time.

An important question in writing this section of your résumé is how far back to reach for relevant experience. Be reasonable. If you held an internship in college for a marketing firm and think you might do something related to that work, it's probably safe to include it. Inversely, it may stretch plausibility too far if you suggest that you learned about business operations from a summer job managing the reception desk at an outdoor pool.

I learned that lesson the hard way. When I tried to cite that very experience in an interview, the hiring manager shot me a furrowed brow and asked a follow-up question that I was unable to answer. While I may have learned valuable lessons in that role, I knew nothing about finance, analytics-driven process optimization, change management, or any of the other concepts I needed to qualify for work as an operations consultant.

The third section of your résumé should include volunteer positions and service roles you held in your professional associations. If your function is self-explanatory, leave it as is; otherwise, use a bullet or two to describe what you accomplished. Just make sure you tell your reader something they want to know. Nobody will care that you pay dues to the Modern Language Association, but many people will view a role on a local leadership council as evidence that peers trust you in positions of responsibility.

Education should be the last section on your résumé—unless your advanced degree genuinely qualifies you for a job or you've been instructed to put that section first. This structure will hopefully prevent readers from dismissing you as over-qualified before reading your work history and skills. When you portray the details of your academic experience, use terms that a nonacademic audience will understand. Omit your thesis title and advisor under your degrees, but cite any awards or honors you received at each level of study, even if they seem silly or superfluous. Although few readers will really know what those accolades mean, they'll use them to judge whether you were successful in your chosen arena.

Fellowships and grants warrant special mention. These awards are so standard in some disciplines that they seem beneath mentioning. In my old field, for example, it's extremely rare to pursue an advanced degree without a tuition waiver and stipend. Many people consequently leave those honors off their CV entirely.

When writing a résumé, it's a grievous error to omit paid fellowships. Many people who dismiss academia (and particularly those who frown upon the humanities and social sciences) view the pursuit of an advanced degree as the acquisition of debt without a way to pay it off. Making clear that you *made money* attending grad school helps to forestall that bias—and to explain why you opted to earn an advanced degree instead of entering the workforce right out of undergrad.

Patricia Soler put many of these strategies into action while seeking work beyond the academy. Since the job she was applying for with the US government required her résumé to list her education first, she turned that section into a powerful statement of her accomplishments and qualifications:

EDUCATION

Georgetown University - Department of Spanish and Portuguese   **Washington, DC**

PhD, Latin American Literature and Cultural Studies (GPA: 3.78/4.00)   **Jan 2014**

MS/BA, Spanish   **May 2004**

- Fellowships: 7-year paid doctoral fellowship; and 1-year paid Foreign Language and Area Studies Fellowship for Portuguese.
- Grants: 12 academic conference grants; 1 research grant for 3-month dissertation study in Brazil; 1 grant for study at Rare Book School, U. of Virginia; hand-selected by Library President for 1st-ever grant to promote original source material research.
- Publications: 1 peer-reviewed article; 2 library catalogues; 1 article on foreign policy; and 1 book review on public policy.
- Project Manager: Hand-selected by the former Provost of Georgetown University for a Mellon-funded grant to create a methodology to assess quality and usefulness of Google Books for academics (publication forthcoming in 2014); monitored data results for 2nd researcher.
- Grant writer + fundraiser: Identified new areas of revenue and raised over $20,000 as Co-Chair of graduate student conference (20% increase from prior year's funds).
- Panel speaker: 12 academic conferences, including the prestigious Modern Language Association Conference, the Brazilian American Studies Association Conference, and the International Conference on the Book.
- Media appearance: Interviewed by NPR to discuss original research findings (2008).

The success of this section derives from the economy with which it portrays academic details (three degrees in two lines, impressive GPAs) and the emphasis it gives to skills that are relevant to bureaucratic management. Patricia quickly demonstrates that she can bring in money, write effectively, manage projects, and speak before both generalist and expert audiences. Her layout also allows her to highlight multiple accomplishments in each of these categories—turning her education into a tour de force that stamps out any doubt about the relevance of her doctoral work to nonacademic employment.

The guidelines I've provided in this section will help you structure a succinct résumé that doesn't prejudice readers against you because of your advanced degree. Even so, break those rules when they don't work for you. If a service or volunteer role is highly relevant to a job you want, list it first in your work history. If you have to start your résumé with education (as Patricia did), turn that constraint to your advantage.

Also remember that some experiences and accomplishments won't make the cut. Unless you're applying for a job as a writer or editor, contain your academic publications to bullets within your work history. If you can speak any foreign languages, name them in your skills list—but only if you're fluent enough to have a conversation. It's also prudent to omit scholarly side projects that aren't relevant to your professional future. For about two years, I translated Italian descriptions of Latin works and authors into English for an initiative in Europe. Unfortunately, I'm not able to *converse* in Italian, and my knowledge of academic jargon doesn't help me in business. As far as my résumé is concerned, those two hundred pages of professional translation never happened.

Translating Your Academic Experience

Thus far I've recommended a generic framework for your résumé (summary, skills, work history, volunteering experience, and education) and advised you to use bullets to flesh out individual roles with meaningful accomplishments. The challenge is that audiences differ in how they define "meaningful." Unless your scholarly experience resonates with professionals in business, academic administration, politics, or nonprofit management, your résumé isn't going to hold your readers' attention—and isn't going to help you get a job.

While it's possible in some cases for me to offer prescriptive guidance on how to translate academic experience for nonacademics, it would be a fool's errand to attempt an exhaustive treatment. Scholarly fields differ widely in their knowledge sets, skills, and methodologies—and my experience is limited to an obscure discipline in the humanities.

What I *can* do in those situations is explain how I undertook this effort myself. By letting you see inside my workshop, as it were, I will outline a process that you can imitate to decipher industry-specific meaning from your own story.

This section takes up the rest of the chapter. For ease of reading, I've broken it up along the three legs of the so-called tenure stool: teaching, service, and research.

TEACHING

When you tell people that you are or wanted to be a professor, most will think of you as a teacher first. Remember that numerous assumptions come with that notion. They'll likely imagine you living a cushy life, working nine hours a week, and enjoying extended summers free of responsibility. As misguided as this vision may be, it's understandable: people who've only expe-rienced school from the students' side of the classroom rarely think about professors beyond that context.

To explain how teaching is relevant in other professional arenas, you'll have to overcome this cultural stereotype. For-tunately, this aspect of your academic life is one of the most complex and varied—and the one you can milk the most once somebody gives you the benefit of the doubt.

In my estimation, you need to master five skills to be a good teacher: project management, public speaking, running meetings, balancing stakeholder interests, and emotional intel-ligence.[6] Let's go through each in turn.

———

Project management is the act of taking a general plan, detailing what you have to do for it to be successful, and mapping those requirements onto a schedule that gives you sufficient time to complete the work while meeting known deadlines. It requires a methodical mind adept at moving between the big picture and minute details, as well as an ability to learn basic concepts quickly. Most of all, it takes the discipline to get project phases back on track when delays in one work stream threaten to slow down dependent efforts.

As an educator, you sharpen these skills every day. Before you set foot in your classroom at the start of the semester, you know what you're going to do for the next sixteen weeks. If you wrote the syllabus, you figured out what you wanted your

6. Rogers (2015) ¶29ff. describes the areas where employees with advanced degrees and their employers thought "alt-ac" professionals needed further training. Her observations on project management suggest this is a skill academics should be careful not to overstate.

students to learn by the end of term and allotted that material to the time available. That effort likely required hard choices to cut topics you wanted to cover or to stretch out less rich content to maintain an even pace.

There's of course still much to do after mocking up that plan. You need to select the most effective way to teach what you want your students to learn, whether through readings, exercises, tests, or less traditional projects. Variety is crucial. As every teacher knows, holding your students' attention enables them to learn—and makes it easier to assess their knowledge and skills. Yet even figuring out what to assess requires a careful balancing act. You don't just need to identify what *you* think students should learn in a given course, but must fit your material into larger program outcomes and university initiatives.

All this work needs to happen before you can script lectures, make slideshows, budget time to grade, and decide when to hold office hours—to say nothing of actually *teaching*. So it's safe to say you know how to plan. And when it comes to execution, you can manage with the best of them. Academics routinely teach multiple courses, covering the topics they planned to convey in spite of delays caused by blizzards, student questions, or—as was the case for me—classes being cancelled to accommodate a football game.

With all of that experience, it's reasonable to claim you're a master of project management. Convincing others of this fact will just require a few anecdotes to show how you applied these skills in an actual setting—and reassurance that you can carry these skills over once you've learned the basics of a new profession.

———

Next is public speaking. This skill is one of the more obvious ones you possess, but it's important to remind people just how often you do it. If you teach full time at the college level, you spend at least eight hours each week in front of a crowd. You know how to throw energy into a room, how to react when a question comes out of left field, and how to make sure you get through a presentation on time. In fact, you speak against a clock so often that you can likely sense when you have five minutes remaining, regardless of how long you've been given.

This experience is impressive on its own, but you can also speak in front of radically different audiences. Sometimes you need to explain material to beginners in a subject, breaking down every concept you discuss. On other occasions, you sit around a seminar table with people whose depth of knowledge mirrors or even exceeds your own. So it isn't just that you know how to lead a large group through scripted material: it's that you know how to tailor information to discrete audiences and move seamlessly between them.

And let's not forget about the entertainment part of this equation. Much of your job, after all, is convincing teens to get excited about subject matter that doesn't interest them. Teachers are expert at turning the mundane into the magical. This skill isn't just a sleight of hand—it's marketable. Most of the work organizations do isn't exciting. They rely on people with enthusiasm and charisma to break through skepticism and get their message across. Whether success means winning a new client, getting a donor to make a large gift, or persuading constituents to vote, teachers are up to the task.

Don't be afraid to lay this on thick when you tell people about your teaching. The pitch I used played on assumptions about my academic field and the city where I live. While I mixed it up a bit depending on my audience, it always went roughly like this:

I've spent three years convincing college students in New Orleans to memorize names and dates from Roman history instead of going out on Bourbon Street. If I can do that, I can sell anything to anyone.

Formulations like this might be hyperbolic, but they're an effective way to convey how your teaching experience is transferable to unexpected contexts.

————

Managing meetings is another skill you may not realize you developed through teaching. In fact, you demonstrate it every time you lead a class discussion: you set an agenda, arrange the room, put key points on the whiteboard, and give a final summary that keeps everyone on the same page. But as you likely know quite well, facilitating a conversation is about more than these mechanics. It's about being able to guide a group with probing questions instead of telling participants what to think—and adapting on the fly when people aren't prepared. In short, it's about letting others believe they're in the driver's seat while working imperceptibly to keep them on the road.

Most graduate students and early career professors have extensive experience in this area. If you're among them, you know what it takes to prepare for a conversation and probably have a sense of why the Socratic method is so effective. The simple truth is that people are more willing to accept a conclusion when they've contributed to the discussion that produces it.

Outside of academia, this outcome is called "stakeholder alignment," and it's perhaps the most critical element of a project's success. If people don't agree about a plan—or think they've been cut out of the process that led to it—work can get delayed or derailed very quickly. People who are able to produce alignment are thus valuable assets to any team.

In order to bridge the gap between "leading a discussion section" and "managing a meeting," consider talking about this skill in more abstract terms. I've come to think of it as the art of engineering discussions that orient people to a shared understanding or goal, even when I don't know what the outcome will look like. In truth, the humanities and social sciences are ideal training grounds for such endeavors: when you've helped people agree about a topic as vague as the meaning of literature, tackling concrete subjects is a cakewalk.

—

Academics are also skilled at balancing stakeholder interests. Any time you walk into a classroom, you're influenced by the competing needs, desires, and requirements of the various groups who have an interest in your work. An example will make this clear.

When a student is going to fail your course, you have to weigh what's best for at least five different stakeholders before deciding how to act:

> **The student.** They usually think it's in their best interest to pass so they can graduate on time and keep their parents happy. Even if they haven't done the work, they'll push aggressively for this outcome. But they aren't in college to pass—they're in college to *learn*. What's best for them might be withdrawing from your course to focus on others, or even accepting a failing mark so there's a real consequence that forces them to learn from their mistakes.
>
> **The department.** Enrollment usually determines budgets. That means urging the student to withdraw or

failing them can harm your entire department. Yet passing them may also have negative consequences: the student might believe they deserved the grade and enroll in an upper-level course they're not prepared for. Not only might that lead them to the same situation again, it would pass the burden to one of your colleagues.

The college. A default expectation today is that colleges want as many students to pass as possible. After all, graduation rate is a key metric on which colleges are ranked, and more alumni means a bigger donor base (at least in the United States, where even public schools rely on donations). But those short-term gains are offset by long-term losses. If you pass enough students who don't have the proficiency their degree is supposed to signify, the college will see its reputation deteriorate over time. That trend may jeopardize the school's ability to attract good students or teachers, its students' ability to take pride in what they accomplish, and its alumni's ability to find work on the merits of their degree.

The field. Depending on the level of the student, your academic discipline might also be implicated. Having more majors, masters, or even PhDs is usually positive: it puts the ideas of your discipline into society, justifies higher levels of funding, and produces a bigger pool of potential teachers or members of the field's professional society. But if these people haven't mastered the content, tools, and methods of your field, they're likely to do more harm than good. Perception of your discipline by the general public might fall, or the individual might become an ineffective teacher who actively weakens the next generation of scholars.

Yourself. The easiest thing for you is undoubtedly to pass the student. It will mean less work and let you get back to other priorities. But doing so might affect your reputation. Other students could learn you're a pushover, and you'll have a hard time saying no to them after letting one student skate through. Moreover, you have a professional obligation to act in the best interests of the above stakeholders. That duty stands whether you benefit from the outcome or not, and a miscalculation could result in blowback or even bad press from which it's hard for you to recover.

This common scenario turns out to be more complicated than it may initially appear. The chief problem I see is that you don't know where to place your first duty of loyalty: every stakeholder can reasonably claim to be the most important, and any action you take has positive and negative ramifications for each one. It doesn't help that colleges rarely have policies on how professors should resolve these tensions. You're usually left to feel them out on your own.

In figuring out how to act, you have to read the political temperature at your college and assess how your actions will ripple across the impacted stakeholders. There isn't any safety in making the "right" call: no such thing exists. Instead, your ability to weather any storm that arises will depend on how you justify your decision to privilege some stakeholders' needs and wants above those of others.

The odds are good that you've faced a situation like this as an academic. While you might not have broken it down as extensively as I did, you no doubt developed some criteria to make up your mind.

Once again, thinking in abstract terms is the first step in translating academic experience into a "transferable skill."

Every organization needs to break down problems, assess political risk, and protect itself from blowback. That fact is as true for a company about to serve a new market as it is for a nonprofit selecting a keynote speaker for their annual gala. Demonstrating that you can think critically about abstract problems and devise a system to decide between multiple bad options will give potential employers confidence that you can protect the organization—and suggest that you'll embrace the mantra Do No Harm as you go about your work.

———

Emotional intelligence (sometimes called EQ, analagous with IQ) is the last skill I'll discuss in this section. This attribute is a hot topic in business right now, and while it's rarely a trait that will get you hired on its own, it may well be one that differentiates you from other candidates—and gives a manager the confidence to hire you.

Although the stereotype casts professors as doddering old men who can't read social cues, the modern academy requires you to be highly sensitive to the people around you. On any given day, you move between novices in your field and experts much your senior, between teens and septuagenarians. The social expectations of these groups vary widely, and it's incumbent on you to operate smoothly and effectively across all of them.

Your work with students both inside and outside the classroom also trains you in this area. While lecturing you need to gauge when people are paying attention and when they're nodding off, and to continue your lesson plan or pivot in real time. Likewise, your one-on-one sessions with students who need extra help have taught you how to deliver negative feedback kindly and to find different ways to explain the same concept. Most importantly, you've learned to guide people towards success without just doing things for them. And since the trend in today's universities is that professors serve as the front line of mental-health support, you've likely learned how to get a baseline reading of people's behavior and spot warning signs when they're under stress.

In short, you're likely to be more in tune to other people—and more adaptable to diverse social situations—than many outside academia will expect. Be sure to show this attribute off by sharing anecdotes that highlight interpersonal interactions, especially if your deft navigation of choppy waters led to a positive outcome.

————

To sum up, your teaching experience has likely given you a range of skills that are marketable beyond the academy. Five that most educators develop are facility for project management, comfort with public speaking, the ability to run meetings, a capacity for balancing stakeholder dynamics, and a depth of emotional intelligence. These attributes can bring out the best in any organization—and put you in a strong position to thrive once you've become familiar with a new work environment.

SERVICE

Service—that is, administrative duties you've taken on for your department, college, or discipline—is another facet of academic life that imbues skills that are useful in the world beyond it. Unfortunately, many academics overlook this type of work and fail to mine it when seeking to convey the value they can bring to nonacademic settings.

To overcome this blind spot, it helps to be mindful about identifying activities that qualify. Start by listing all the academic work that prevents you from teaching and research. Your items might include writing committee reports for the faculty senate, organizing a grad student conference, or overseeing a department's guest lecture schedule. Once you've assembled your list, go through each role and assess which ones you enjoy doing as well as those you don't.

If you're in a "tenure-trap" job or looking to leave a tenure-track role, you likely have a wealth of experience in this area. Graduate students and contingent faculty may not be so lucky. As temporary fixtures at your college, you're often precluded from business that falls under the umbrella of "self-governance." Even so, make the most of positions you've held, and if you find a role you'd like to explore, try to talk your way into it despite your "visiting" status.

Next, ask yourself *why* you like certain jobs and dislike others. Be specific. If you have mixed feelings about a position, try to parse out which tasks are engaging and which ones bore or annoy you. Doing so will allow you to focus on experience that excites you, which you'll naturally convey to other people with greater enthusiasm.

Once you've narrowed down your service experience, imagine how you would describe it to a nonacademic audience. Be sure to include one or two anecdotes that explain both how you succeeded in the role and what personal traits enabled you to be so effective. From now on, bring these experiences up in your informational interviews and refine how you pitch them based on the reactions you receive.

——

Since it would be impossible to explain how to translate any imaginable service role you might have held into terms that are meaningful to nonacademic audiences, I'll provide a detailed treatment of a single role from my own experience. In particular, I'll explain how I present my work as chair of the Society for Classical Studies' Contingent Faculty Committee. This position was so interesting to me—and relatable to people outside academia—that it displaced my job as a visiting assistant professor as the first experience entry on my résumé.

This time let's start with the final product and an explanation of what it tries to accomplish. Afterwards, I'll provide a narrative account of the experience that served as raw material for the summary and break down why I selected specific details from it.

2015–2018: Society for Classical Studies
Chair, Contingent Faculty Committee
Chair, Advisory Committee on Non-Tenure-Track Faculty
*   Issues*

Over the course of three years, I transformed a twenty-person advisory group in my professional society into a standing committee that won a series of gains and protections for contingent faculty. These included changes to our professional ethics statement and creation of a new travel fund. My accomplishments were revenue-neutral and stayed within the organization's limited purview. Critical to the success I achieved was my ability to:

- Align people with divergent viewpoints around common goals
- Execute long-term strategies in clear, sequential phases
- Recognize the strengths of my team and delegate work accordingly
- Persuade skeptics to embrace politically sensitive objectives

This description is designed to give most people everything they need to know about my role and the work I did within it: it states my achievements, gives a sense of their scale and cost, and summarizes how I personally got them done. It also highlights the set of skills that I believe are most likely to carry over to other contexts: alignment, project planning and execution, delegation, and stakeholder management. To make sure my reader doesn't miss any of these points, I've conveyed each skill using a single bullet, a format that draws the eye better than a wall of text.

Admittedly, it took multiple revisions to craft this simple and coherent summary. Since I knew the details of the work—as well as how long efforts took or how hard they were to accomplish—it was initially difficult for me to highlight meaningful information over extraneous data. The fuller account of this work provided below will make this point clear. As you read, compare that narrative to the version above, considering the specific details I chose to extract as well as how I put them into nonacademic terms.

The president of my professional society convened an advisory group on non-tenure-track faculty issues in 2015. When I joined we had no defined leader and an obscure mandate. As a result, our email exchanges were disorganized. Some people wanted to form a union, and others lamented that tenured faculty and society at large didn't give us the value or respect we deserved. There was no clear direction—just vented anger and shots in the dark.

It seemed clear to everyone that proceeding in that way wouldn't produce a viable path forward. So when a call came for someone to take charge of the group, I volunteered.

In truth I didn't think I was qualified. At that point I'd held my doctorate for less than a year and had only spent a few months in a contingent role. Fortunately for me, most academics are reserved. Only one other person threw their hat in the ring—and said they would pass on the job if anybody else offered to take it.

I thus found myself at the head of an advisory group for a national organization before I'd turned thirty. I had absolutely no idea what I was doing—or what to do. But I had three things on my side: enthusiasm, a "light" 3–3 teaching load, and the awareness that we couldn't solve any problems yet because we hadn't defined them.

My first act as the group's leader was to choose a secretary to keep us organized. The woman who volunteered was active in our discussions, and as I later learned was the other person who had expressed interest in serving as de facto chair. She also had experience using Google Docs and setting up shared worksites—and in a past life had built surveys and run analytics for a marketing firm.

After she got those tools up and running, I set about convincing the group to act as one by focusing on discrete parts of the problem at hand. This task was bigger than it seemed. In order to do it, I allotted six months for us to collectively assess how non-tenure-track faculty fared in different areas of their professional lives. We took these issues one by one, sharing personal anecdotes and articles on systemic problems. We also polled the society's membership on how they saw contingent faculty making out at their colleges in order to produce broad quantitative data for our field. After all this was done, I compiled a report that summarized our findings. This document provided a shared understanding and gave us a common basis for determining next steps.

We spent the second half of that academic year hammering out real solutions. I divided our members into working groups and assigned each one an area to assess. Although I gave them broad leeway to recommend whatever they saw fit, I reminded them that viable solutions had to be pragmatic, cost nothing, and fall within our limited scope of action. By early May, we agreed on five goals we thought the Society should pursue that would pave the way for better treatment of contingent faculty. I then drafted a brief that included a condensed version of the problems we identified the prior fall and explanations of the solutions we wanted to implement. After getting feedback from the group and making final revisions, I submitted our report to the Society's board.

Our accomplishments over the course of that first year apparently impressed them. The board accepted our recommendation that the advisory group be converted to a standing committee at the start of the next calendar year— an outcome that would allow us to pursue the goals we'd established and take on new ones in the future. Furthermore, they freed up money from another source to provide travel grants for contingent faculty to attend the Society's annual conference. We hadn't asked for this, but our report convinced them this critical issue had to be addressed as soon as possible.

The only negative result of this victory was that we had to hew more closely to the Society's bylaws. That meant our group shrank from twenty members to six when the committee became permanent. Fewer people meant fewer labor hours, so we decided to focus on just two of the initiatives we had recommended to the board that spring.

Our chief concern was amending the Society's professional ethics statement to cover treatment of contingent faculty. This process was long and complex: we had to propose edits, secure buy-in from the relevant vice president, and put the revised version of the ethics statement up to the general membership for a vote. All told, it took about eighteen months, but it finally came back in our favor.

By that time, my term as chair was nearly done. After organizing a single meeting of my counterparts in other disciplines and brainstorming ways to work together, I passed the baton to my successor so he could see our mission through.

I'll go out on a limb and guess that you've been bored for the last few minutes. If so, it's with good reason. As I've said before, most people don't care about the interior lives of others—they care about how other people's experiences are relevant to them.

But let's be more precise. Apart from brevity, the big difference in my accounts is what narratologists call "focalization"—the perspective that a speaker or author adopts in telling a story. The long account I just finished offers an *internal* view: it emphasizes how I felt, why I acted, and what I responded to at each step in the process. Although I know those details of my work intimately, they're necessarily invisible: you can't see them or even confirm that they're an accurate reflection of my experience. All you can do is take my word for it.

On the other hand, the résumé version of this role offers an *external* perspective. I quickly tell you about my most significant accomplishments and convey that I achieved them through my personal strengths. While space constraints don't allow me to prove any of these claims, they can all be verified through a reference or mutual contact. They consequently appear credible—and inspire confidence that my summary is more than idle boasting.

"But wait," you may be thinking, "you didn't do those things by yourself! You had a team of people do them for you. How can you take credit for their work?"

This critique is valid—to a point. The people I worked with undertook most of the committee's heavy lifting, and I wouldn't have been a tenth as effective without them. But the target audience of my résumé doesn't know the organization I worked for or the people involved. They're reading to learn about me, to see what I've done, and hopefully to get a sense of what I can do for them. I've consequently focused on successes I can *plausibly* lay claim to, including orchestration of the group's efforts and the accomplishments we achieved under my direction. Given that I *did* lead the committee, this obfuscation is minor—and in any case accords with a key expectation of the résumé genre: that you trumpet your own achievements.

———

Service positions often provide your most relatable experience. They give many academics the opportunity to develop leadership skills, steer initiatives through rough waters, and otherwise hone capacities and build knowledge in matters unrelated to scholarship. Best of all, they frequently allow you to manage a budget, which is a skill that is instantly recognizable—and valuable—to people in any sector. Whatever service roles you choose to emphasize from your own experience, just remember to cast them in *external* terms—and to make their relevance as obvious as possible.

RESEARCH

Odds are good that the day-to-day activities of your research are hard to explain. They tend to be highly specialized, repetitive, and don't look like work to most outsiders. Those of you in the sciences are lucky: long hours in the lab are what nonacademics think of first when they hear the word "research." Other civilians might imagine running polls for a project in the social sciences or mining archives as a historian, but those few vignettes nearly exhaust the word's valances in the popular imagination. As a result, you may struggle to explain how you've spent the last five to ten years to people who aren't already in the know.

I break research into two classes of activity. The first covers studies in the lab, field, or library, including the methods and tools you use to do that work. The second covers writing—that is, translating your studies into a form that people can access and understand without your intervention.

———

Since writing is easier to deal with, let's tackle it first. As an academic, you've spent countless hours composing seminar papers, theses, articles, case studies, even monographs. Regardless of the form scholarship takes in your discipline, writing requires you to convert complex ideas into accurate and unambiguous prose.

It may come as a surprise to learn that the precision you use when getting ideas out of your head and onto a page is extremely rare. People outside academia tend to have lots of words and phrases that convey the same concept. In my experience, professionals are especially fond of metaphors from war, athletics, and gambling—and frequently use the first one that comes to mind or the last one that was mentioned. Completeness and accuracy of thought are rare.[7]

7. For a fuller and more humorous assessment of this phenomenon, see Molly Young's "Garbage Language: Why Do Corporations Speak the Way They Do?," *Vulture*, February 20, 2020: https://www.vulture.com/2020/02/spread-of-corporate-speak.html.

When this manner of conveying information works, it's decidedly efficient. And it does work most of the time. But when it fails, communication grinds to a halt, along with forward progress on whatever effort is at hand. The most common culprits I've spotted during my time in business include the following:

- Phrases that sound one way in the author's head, but read differently on the page
- References to obscure events, people, or cultural touchstones
- Unfamiliar or unintelligible idioms

Academic writers assiduously avoid these pitfalls. We may not always be concise, but we're trained to write unambiguous prose that's designed to last. This skill is especially valuable when business is increasingly conducted online and the workforce grows more global every day.

Another attribute you possess from years of research is the ability to apply a style guide quickly and evenly. Consistency is the polish that allows organizations to present a clean image of their brand to the outside world—and a skill that anyone who's written a thesis or published an article is likely to possess. This attribute is valuable in any role, but especially for writing-intensive positions in communications or marketing.

In a broader sense, your research also shows that you can devise a long-term project, break it into parts, and execute it successfully with minimal oversight. Although I spoke about project management in the "Teaching" section, it bears expansion here.

Your dedication to academic research proves beyond any shadow of a doubt that you're a self-starter with strong intrinsic motivation. After all, you've built your career on figuring out where scholarship is deficient and devising ways to solve thorny problems. That trait is part of who you are, and it's something you're going to bring to any table you sit at. It also makes you stand out: many people are content to do what they're told and wait for specific instructions before acting. Those who take the initiative to fill obvious gaps and make less work for their superiors often get ahead.

Academics likewise tend to know whether the tool we're applying to solve a problem is the right one—and if not, where we might go to find a better approach. In fact, this is something David Stevens says he couldn't have learned anywhere besides higher education.

The friends David had at Princeton weren't just political scientists like he was. They did cybernetics, anthropology, and economics—weird and diverse subjects that he struggled to understand. But that experience had a significant impact on David's personal development. It taught him how people in different fields think and approach problems, making him cognizant of the gaps in his own knowledge and sensitive to how other professionals could apply their unique talents to solve complex problems.

Since leaving academia, David has come to recognize the value of this experience more and more. He's found that many colleagues in business and policy are uncomfortable being proved wrong in front of a group. This reflex is partly understandable: professional reputations depend on credibility, so many people are skittish around information that challenges their position. Unfortunately, this aversion can sometimes go too far, leading people to ignore valid counterevidence or advance recommendations that are insufficiently nuanced.

David's exposure to and comfort with other ways of thinking have inured him to this weakness. He never feels like he needs to tamp down new approaches and knows where to find effective or efficient methodologies to tackle the challenges before him. In a world where results matter, this openness has become a source of power that differentiates him in the market.

While project management and its related problem-solving skills are practiced across higher education, those of you in the sciences may have an advantage in speaking about your experience. Since your research often involves teams of people—and you may have overseen assistants directly—you can describe your responsibilities in *managerial* terms that are instantly intelligible to audiences outside academia.

It's also possible to turn your long tenure as a student into a positive. While in academia, you spent years making sense of complex, murky, and often contradictory information—and before you could specialize in your area of expertise, you had to learn a vast amount of general knowledge about your field. Many of those topics will have been unfamiliar when you began, and you probably found some of them downright boring. This experience nevertheless highlights an important trait: you're extremely good at learning new subjects quickly. You do it every day, often without even thinking about it.

Not so sure? Every grad student I know has a story of lecturing on material they had to learn on short notice. Maybe you had to explain race in colonial America for a sick colleague or teach Mesopotamian flood myths for an on-campus interview. Whatever the details, you had to dive into a subject you didn't know well, figure out the basics, and present a coherent narrative in a public forum on short notice.

Outside of academia, there's a constant need for this skill and a constant shortage of people who can do it well. Take pride in your ability to learn quickly, and use it to stand out in the marketplace. As long as someone knowledgeable points you in the right direction, you can quickly "get smart" on a competitive landscape, future opportunities for a client, or anything else an organization needs to be briefed on.

———

What about your actual area of expertise? Marketing your academic knowledge and skills is another place where you'll have to do the hard work yourself. Even so, I can offer a few tips to point you in the right direction.

Let's start with a basic definition. At its heart, research is an iterative process (re-) of seeking specific information about an issue (-search). The practice entails two distinct tasks: (1) analyzing data in a structured and critical way, and (2) assessing the relative strengths of major strands of thought about that data. The breakthrough that (hopefully) emerges from these efforts gets most of the attention, but it's really just a byproduct. After all, to devise a new approach to an old problem, you have to understand why earlier solutions failed.

Fields differ in how they conduct this type of assessment, and the specific tools and approaches they employ mark them as distinct areas of study. This is why we call them disciplines: those who are practiced in a given area habitually conduct their work according to set standards. Seen in this light, research becomes more accessible. Even if most people outside academia won't understand *what* you study, they are likely capable of grasping *how* you go about your work.

To show you how to translate even the most arcane of skills into terms that make sense outside of higher ed, I'll use my research as an example. The main tool I used as an academic is called philology (i.e., "love of words or reason"). Essentially, it's a technique for uncovering large, thematic issues in a work of literature through close reading and careful analysis of the language that makes it up. The process of philological analysis is highly structured and requires you to view a text at multiple levels:

1. The individual words that are used, how the author deploys them elsewhere, and how they're used by other authors
2. How words fit together to form scenes, where those scenes fit within a larger work, and whether parallel scenes in literary predecessors or successors shed light on what the author was trying to convey
3. Whether the author's cultural or historical context invites other interpretations or creates the potential for subtexts that cut against the surface meaning
4. How those words, scenes, parallels, contexts, and subtexts either contribute to or fight against the general progression or tone of the narrative

The content of this research doesn't interest most people, but conducting such analysis for over a decade made me adept at evaluating the written word. I learned to gauge how language affects its readers and how subtle changes to words or word order can provoke a different response. Along the way, I developed a vocabulary to describe rhetorical devices with precision. This knowledge allows me to explain why certain turns of phrase are powerful or others are ungrammatical. Crucially, I can apply the philological framework I learned in academia to any writing composed in a language and culture that I know. Roman epic poetry was just the whetstone I used to sharpen my tools.

To put the matter more simply, classics trained me to assess and deconstruct persuasive speech. After ten years of practice, that habit became a reflex. As I move about the world, I'm constantly eyeing grammatical mistakes, critiquing odd turns of phrase, and thinking of ways to make them better. I cringe when an advertisement misses the mark or a TV script falls flat—and make a game of trying to pinpoint where the writers went wrong.

The relevance of these skills to strategic communications should be obvious. I know how to break down language quickly and rephrase it to be simpler and more effective. I consider not just what words mean, but where they fit within a larger context and how they're likely to be perceived by my target audience. This skill allows me to put the benefits of a new technology in terms that make sense to a chief financial officer or to tell a chief marketing officer how different accounting ledgers free up time for more valuable work. In short, I'm a master translator who can convey an organization's strengths to a range of audiences.

Make no mistake: describing my academic skills so clearly wasn't easy. It took me two years of trial and error before I could do it well enough to land a job, and even today I struggle to get it right every time my academic past comes up. But you don't need to be perfect. As long as you can make a plausible case that your research skills are interesting and relevant beyond the lab or library, you'll eventually get a hiring manager on your side.

To do this faster than I did, pay attention to a few details. First, separate *how* you conduct your research from the minutiae of *what* you study. My academic work taught me to move rapidly from small details to the big picture—or to use a metaphor from the ancient world, to see both the mosaic and its tiles. Although I didn't realize it when I was a classicist, this skill is extremely rare: many of the professionals I work with today can only do one or the other.

The catch is that I'll never get a chance to convey that I can do both if the first thing I tell a nonexpert is that I worked on a poem about Roman civil war. The situation only gets worse if I dive into the words, characters, and ancient philosophies I spent years trying to make sense of. Conversation of that sort is alienating. Instead, explain your research approach in the broadest, most basic terms available—and demonstrate how the methods and tools you use produce a meaningful insight.

Second, be strategic in how you try to sell yourself. Before you sit down to meet with someone, make an educated guess about the skills they value and try to frame your experience in terms that will resonate. I refined my message only after I'd narrowed my search to jobs in communications, operating on the assumption that recruiters in that field would care about my sensitivity to readers and language. While I might not have fronted those specific skills when applying for a different job or discussing my scholarship inside academia, it was an effective choice for my target audience.

You can't expect to be good at translating your research experience right away. Work through each of your skills from this arena in turn, practice describing them in informational interviews, and refine your description of them as often as it takes to strike on something that's persuasive. With enough time and polish, you're sure to make the story you tell about your research shine.

A Model Résumé

It's time to see how this advice looks when it all comes together. The following résumé comes from an anthropology PhD who asked for anonymity because of the sensitive nature of their current work. To respect that request, I've called them "Taylor" and used obviously playful titles for their employers, educational institutions, and publications. Otherwise, the résumé below hews close to their accomplishments and how they describe them:

Taylor Sloed, Ph.D.

Turning everyday insights into accelerated impact

EXPERIENCE

UX Researcher, Macrosoft
JANUARY 2019 - PRESENT

- Identified new critical user journeys for PolyProduct through reviews of internal and external research
- Established the criteria and protocols for a new PolyProduct evaluation using usability studies, remote studies, and café studies
- Developed empathy-building exercises for stakeholders leading ethnographic in-home visits for foundational PolyProduct research
- Evaluated new metrics for PolyProduct enterprise platforms

Postdoctoral Researcher, University of California, West Covina
SEPTEMBER 2018 - DECEMBER 2018

- Directed a ten-minute ethnographic film on one family's relationships with birds and death in Buenos Aires
- Finished the book manuscript for Pigeon Hunters (Puffin 2019) and wrote an invited article on Argentinian bird watchers

Postdoctoral Researcher, Universidad Nacional de Argentina
SEPTEMBER 2016 - AUGUST 2018

- Taught research methods, published an article on financial birders in Argentina, and wrote a prize-winning essay on why Argentinian birders refuse to use binoculars

Graduate Scholar, Sanford University
SEPTEMBER 2010 - SEPTEMBER 2016

- Defended a dissertation based on 24 months of ethnographic fieldwork into how rising Argentinian bird conservators deal with the practical and psychological challenges of climate change

EDUCATION

Sanford University, Palo Alto, CA
Ph.D. in Sociocultural Anthropology
SEPTEMBER 2010 - SEPTEMBER 2016

Thomas Jefferson College, Washington, DC
B.A. in Latin American Studies
SEPTEMBER 2005 - MAY 2009

SKILLS

Ethnography
In-home studies
International research
Research design
Proposal writing
Public speaking
Video editing
Usability testing
Intercept studies
Surveys
Literature reviews

PUBLICATIONS

Pigeon Hunters: An Ethnography (Puffin 2019)
"The Disappearing Parrots" (2018)
"Avian Violence" (2018)
"Birding in Uncertain Times" (2017)
"Fair-feathered Friends" (2017)

LANGUAGES

English (native speaker)
Spanish (fluent)
Portuguese (conversational)

CONTACT

taylor.sloed@jeemail.com
555.867.5309

This résumé works well because it tells a simple story through a sleek, modern layout that's reminiscent of a website. Since most people get their information online, this choice makes it feel familiar and easy to digest.

But what about the details? Let's start with what draws the eye first: the name. The oversized font makes it easy to spot in a stack of papers—and invites you to read the tagline printed below. This pithy phrase packs a lot into a small space. It suggests both that Taylor is an expert at observing the world around them and flags their interest in applying those observations to solve real problems quickly.

The bullets on their current role—a temporary position in the tech industry—are also good. They show experience conducting research in multiple contexts, as well as an ability to teach observation methods to other people. While there's no "accomplishment" to suggest how effective Taylor was at these tasks, the summary proves they can perform them in a nonacademic environment. This inclusion is critical: however wrongly, some people will question whether a PhD could "fit in" at their nonacademic organization.

I know that most of you won't be able to get a part-time job at a leading tech company as your primary way of building experience. Even so, this section is useful as a model for how to talk about a service or volunteering role that taught you skills you need for the career you want.

Taylor is also shrewd in their treatment of academic positions. Writing just one or two bullets on each, they focus on accomplishments anyone can appreciate: directing a film, finishing a book, writing a prize-winning essay. They don't hide the fact that they undertook these projects as a grad student, postdoc, or professor—but avoid using the jargon that's typical of academic writing. Taylor also draws a clear line between their work in higher education and skills required for the positions they were seeking (note the words practical, research, financial, ethnographic, climate). Most importantly, each of these attributes shows that Taylor lives their tagline: Turning everyday insights into accelerated impact.

Taylor has placed other details—such as education, languages, and contact information—out of the way. Such secondary content may color the portrait of who Taylor is, but it's not going to get them hired. Giving it better real estate would only have wasted the reader's limited attention.

Also note the aesthetic touches that make this résumé easy to navigate. Taylor has established a clear hierarchy of information by using all capitals to mark section headings and by employing slightly different fonts for their name, their experience and education positions, and the main text. At the same time, the document's two-column design separates longer descriptions from shorter phrases. This layout alleviates the need for printed bullets in the latter section and creates an abundance of white space that keeps the page from feeling crowded. Taken together, these features make it easy for a reader to skim the page and find the information they want.

The fact that most résumés today are viewed on computers or phones instead of print opens further design possibilities. For example, you can use a simple accent color to draw the eye even more quickly to key sections (name, major headings) and employ hyperlinks to direct readers to your published works without spelling out their release date and venue.

Ultimately, Taylor's layout is highly effective for someone who's leaving academia. Note how the first experience item and the list of skills are almost equal in height. The line of white space that this creates draws your eye to the skills immediately after you've read the description of Taylor's current job. While you're there, you don't just see what they believe they're good at: you find keywords that are business-focused and likely to show up on a list of requisite attributes for a particular job. Herein lies the brilliance of the résumé's design: many hiring managers will already know at this point whether they want to schedule an interview—and they haven't even processed that Taylor spent the bulk of their career in academia.

In short, this résumé is a model for someone in your shoes—and one that I chose to adopt even after I'd successfully found a job beyond the professoriate.

Conclusion

This chapter has given you the tools you need to explain to nonacademics why your degree was worth the effort. In truth, reshaping your experience is an essential step in your career transition: since you can't hide the time you spent in higher ed, you need to be able to account for it.

When you get comfortable conveying your skills to new audiences—and can do so consistently and with finesse—you'll know it's time to turn your attention to activities that require a more hands-on approach: developing new strengths beyond the ones you already possess.

Action Items

1. Write an entry in your career journal that consists of just three sentences: an overview of your strengths and interests. Revise that entry weekly until you have a single statement of your professional value.

2. Draft a résumé that translates your academic experience into terms that are intelligible to people in the fields you're interested in.

3. Reach out to a contact you connected with during an informational interview and ask them to critique your first résumé draft.

5

Develop

I spent my first year looking for jobs beyond the classroom focused on college administration. It was a mistake to limit my search so radically. While I would have been happy to end up in one of those roles, refusing to look beyond an industry I already knew considerably lengthened my search for a new career.

But at that point I was still attached to the idea of working in higher education, and I assumed—wrongly—that I could more easily pivot into that area than into business or government. Only after failed attempts to find work in admissions, advancement, and service learning did I finally investigate what jobs were available outside the ivory tower.

As I blinked into the sun of that new world, I was overcome by its size and by my own inadequacy. Two boutique consultancies in New Orleans put employee biographies on their websites. Each included a litany of professional successes, work with charities, leadership forums, and hobbies ranging from music to athletics. These professionals did *everything*— and were good at it, too. Instantly, I could see my résumé the way others did. The accomplishments I'd been so proud of felt small and insignificant.

My conversation with Dan Porterfield—then one year in the past—came back to me in an instant. I realized that I'd only taken part of his advice. Informational interviews and service roles inside the academy had taught me a great deal. But by trying to cling to that world as long as I could, I'd put off an equally important task: doing real work to reinvent myself.

Confronting Your Résumé Gaps

Getting a job takes more than selling academic wares to non-academic buyers. You need to prove to employers that you have concrete skills they can use right away—or at least that you can learn them quickly. For most academics, making a persuasive case means investing time and effort to develop yourself into a more attractive candidate.

You're now in a strong position to do so effectively. Conducting informational interviews and translating your academic skills for new audiences should have taught you where there are gaps in your résumé relative to people who have the jobs you want. You should also have an idea of the roles that will help you fill them—and know how to talk to people who can connect you to new opportunities. What's left is to get to work.

Focusing on skills development will provide an opportunity to ask three questions that are central to this stage in your career transformation:

1. What's the story you want to tell about yourself?
2. Where can you get the experience you need to tell it?
3. How can you use that story to land a new job?

This part of leaving academia is undoubtedly one of the hardest. To develop new skills, you may need to put yourself in positions that you feel are beneath you or even report to someone far your junior. Don't let your ego get in the way of success. Instead, accept that you're no longer the expert in the room and embrace the challenge of learning new skills and acquiring knowledge about new fields. Most of all, remember that this phase of the journey is temporary: once you get a base level of experience in a new area, you're likely to advance much faster than feels possible right now.

Acquiring Skills, Building Experience

There are four practical ways to build your résumé on short notice: online learning, professional training, volunteering, and part-time work.

Let's tackle online learning first. In today's world, it isn't hard to teach yourself basic concepts and tools. The Internet has a wealth of tutorials, do-it-yourself videos, and training courses that are almost always free and allow you to work at your own pace. If you realize you should be able to do something for the jobs you want, go out and learn how to do it.

Productivity software is a good place to start. Microsoft PowerPoint and Excel are ubiquitous in professional settings, serving as the go-to methods for sharing information. At a minimum, know how to create new files and manage basic formatting. People will take this knowledge for granted, and you don't want to be in the awkward position of having to pass off such a simple task to a coworker once you start your new career.

Also know what's possible beyond these basic functions—and consider learning to use the ones that seem most useful. I wrote in Word for over a decade as an academic and thought

I knew it well. It wasn't until I started my current job that I learned about format painter, Shift-F3, and custom styles.[1] These features would have saved me days of effort while editing my dissertation if comfort with the program hadn't led me to stop learning. Don't make the same mistake: twenty minutes on YouTube can save twenty hours of effort.

Depending on your current skills and interests, you might also brush up on other programs. An art historian might practice with Adobe Creative Suite, while a geologist or archaeologist could focus on GIS mapping. In fact, the latter skill helped a friend get a job with a state department of forestry after he initially used it for his research on riverbeds. As long as you have access to a program that's potentially relevant for nonacademic work, you'll be well served by mastering its advanced features.

This advice doesn't mean you should only build on skills you already possess. Rather, I'm suggesting it's okay to grab low-hanging fruit first. If there's a new program or methodology that would be useful for you to master, by all means go out and learn it.

Professional training is another way to develop new knowledge or skills, but programs can vary widely in quality and cost. As a general rule, I would only pay for a course that a networking contact tells me is relevant to a job I want. Prices with a comma are probably too high, unless the course leads to a certification that's a prerequisite in the field you're pursuing. Just remember to check a program's ratings and seek out free equivalents first: some professional training schools are

---

1. Format painter will copy the formatting of the highlighted text and let you "paint" it onto other text, eliminating the need for manual changes. Shift-F3 toggles highlighted text between all lowercase, Title Case, Sentence case, and ALL CAPITALS. Custom styles allow you to automatically format text such as your main copy, titles, subtitles, and inset quotations.

rackets, and you don't want to fall for a scam that puts you in a financial hole.

One type of training that warrants special mention is project management. In the last chapter, I discussed how many academics hone their ability to manage people and work products throughout the course of their doctorate. If you're interested in turning such work into a career, you can make the case more forcefully by seeking a recognized designation such as "Project Management Professional" (PMP) or "Certified Scrum Master" (CSM).

As a current colleague puts it, the PMP certification is prized by organizations that want to impose a greater degree of order and consistency on how they tackle complex work. If you meet the qualifications to apply and have an interest in leading large teams, the course may be worth the investment. CSMs are project managers who receive specialized training to oversee software development—a field that's growing by the day. For those of you who want to work in technology but don't know a coding language, this certification can provide an access point: the latest CSM standards don't require it. Rather, the designation simply attests to your familiarity with leading processes and your ability to keep projects running on time and within budget.

Whether you're considering one of the above certifications or any other formal training, use LinkedIn to determine what's a prerequisite for work you want to do and rely on your network to find out what's worth the effort.

Those of you working for or attending a college may have another way to acquire professional training. Many schools still offer tuition waivers to full-time employees, and graduate students may be entitled to take courses outside their department. Often, you'll be able to find listings in areas like business, public administration, or even law that can teach you critical skills for a new career. Schools of continuing studies are also a good place to look. They tend to offer classes at night—and you won't be the only student of a nontraditional age who's enrolled.

I put this benefit to good use during my last year at Tulane. In order to familiarize myself with basic business concepts, I enrolled in statistics, finance, management, and business law. Apart from what I paid for books, this course of study didn't cost me a dime. There was an added benefit, too. While scanning the requirements for Tulane's School of Professional Advancement, I learned that I qualified for a Certificate in Management. Earning this designation gave my basic proficiency a college's stamp of approval and conveyed to hiring managers that I was serious about changing careers.

If I have one regret about the time I invested in extra training, it's that I thought I was only qualified to take entry-level undergraduate courses. In fact, graduate programs in professional studies don't expect their students to have the same deep knowledge of their subject matter that graduate programs in the arts and sciences do. If you want to enroll in an advanced course in a discipline that's unfamiliar, just email the professor the way you would any other networking contact. Explain your position, tell them why you want to take their course, and ask for a meeting to discuss whether it would be feasible for someone in your position.

Volunteering offers another path to new skills and knowledge. To get started, find a charity that does good work in your community and email the executive director or program leader about supporting their mission. Be forthright: tell them you're building your résumé to enable a career change, and ask if you can support someone who can teach you specific skills you'd like to cultivate. Maybe that's helping their bookkeeper and learning to manage accounts, or perhaps it's contacting donors to track fundraising leads. Even updating a website or running a Facebook account can be good for them and you: they'll be free to focus on work that's more critical to their core mission, and you get experience in digital marketing.

Don't think that volunteering has to represent a significant amount of time to be worth the effort. Of the two charities I supported while searching for a new career, one took two hours a month, and the other about five. This experience was hardly a burden on my schedule. Even so, it allowed me to add two lines to my résumé and gain practical experience in financial strategy, fundraising, and program development. I also got the satisfaction of knowing I'd been able to help my community in the process—and I still support one of those organizations today.

Our last concern in this section is part-time work. This experience is especially valuable because it shows in no uncertain terms that you can succeed beyond the ivory tower. But not all work is created equal. Make sure positions you take on will expand a skill or knowledge set you need in order to embark on a career that's attractive to you. Serving as a tutor or dog walker can pay the bills, but both prevent you from spending time on pursuits that will set you up for new professional roles. Remember: *the opportunity cost of menial work is extremely high.*

I got lucky. A friend with a small IT business hired me to clean up his account books prior to tax filings, to build a new website, and to run a marketing campaign to bring in new clients. I didn't have any background in these areas, but he suspected I could do them well enough—and knew I would accept a lower hourly rate than someone more experienced. After a little prodding, I got over my doubts and said yes. The next six months were great: I got an inside look at what his technology work entailed and learned how to position his company against others in the marketplace.

You don't need to know a business owner to start branching out: for all its faults, the gig economy can be a good friend to someone in your shoes. Every day, companies seek help with projects that require editing, presentation design, video work—really any area where they don't want to pay an expert long-term. They post listings for these jobs on their own webpages, on Craigslist, and even on sites like Upwork and Guru, which are essentially Uber for professional jobs. If you see an activity you might want to try, sign up and enter a bid for the work. Doing so is a low-risk way to build a portfolio you can show employers and to signal that you're an enterprising person who can deliver results in a nonacademic environment.

Personal creative endeavors are a useful addendum to this category of work. Even if a photography site or blog doesn't generate any revenue, the content you create will hone your skills and build your interests—and show them off to a wider public.

Liz Segran learned this during her first few months beyond academia. While still seeking a new career, she decided to pass some free time making jam. There was very little content about that process available online, so Liz started a website to discuss techniques and review products. This endeavor took off: people began to follow her posts, comment on her recipes, and ask her for advice. She was soon managing a new persona online—and even got invited to judge jam for a festival in San Francisco. The irony? *Liz doesn't even care that much about jam.* Her side project had simply taken on a life of its own.

As silly as this story might seem, Liz learned a great deal from her jam blog. She had to design her own website, figure out search engine optimization (SEO, that is, the art of getting your site to come up first on Google and its competitors), manage a social media presence, and tackle a host of other issues related to being the Internet's leading expert on *something*. In short, these skills provided an entry to the career in journalism that Liz subsequently undertook. That path was winding, but eventually led to her dream job as a writer for *Fast Company*, a leading progressive business publication.

My own investments in a personal creative endeavor also paid off. For about six months at the start of 2017, I maintained a blog that discussed contingent faculty issues and chronicled my journey to a new career. More than anything, this forum provided me with a place to ~~talk about my feelings~~ process my thoughts and to practice writing in a colloquial style that was unconstrained by the tics of formal scholarship. I hoped that people might find my musings useful, but never expected them to amount to much.

As it turned out, two organizations considered me for a job while I was engaged in this effort, and both asked me to complete a writing exercise as part of my application. These opportunities came across my desk within two weeks of one another, and each asked for a sample in different genres than I'd composed before. A year earlier, I would have been terrified of this challenge—and even when confronted with it in 2017, I could easily have fallen flat.

But nerves never overtook me. Instead, my practice writing for my blog—and revising the website for my friend's IT business—made these exercises feel easy. I even began to have *fun* trying to persuade an imagined audience with the plain and simple speech I was by then more comfortable using. This feeling was apparently a sign of my skill as much as my enjoyment: both organizations interviewed me on the merits of my writing sample.

One final avenue for finding part-time work is to enlist the aid of a temp agency. This strategy can be efficient, but it requires an entirely different approach from what I advise elsewhere in this book. The jobs you get from a temp agency almost never teach useful skills. Instead, they're a way to get your foot in the door at a company you'd like to work for full-time. Most of these jobs will feel beneath you, and most of them are. But once you're working within an organization, you'll have opportunities to impress people who can recognize your potential. Given the reputation of most temps, it won't be hard to exceed expectations. Seek out people in leadership roles, demonstrate initiative while they're watching, and do whatever it takes to convince them you'd be an asset.

There are two caveats when adopting this strategy. First, temp jobs carry a very high opportunity cost. Quit any position that doesn't provide the access you need to talk your way into a better role—even after one day. Second, the quality of the company and its support system for employees is paramount. Research any organization you're assigned to and prioritize established entities that offer employees self-directed training and preferential treatment for open listings. While you won't qualify for these benefits as a temp, they'll be the avenues you use to advance if you succeed in convincing someone to hire you for a permanent position.

Temp work isn't for the faint of heart. It takes humility, gumption, and effort. In fact, pride prevented me from even considering it when a networking contact told me she'd done it earlier in her career. But former academics *have* made this strategy work for them: David Engel, for instance, used it to find his way from a data-entry cubicle to a managing director's office at Wells Fargo Advisors.

Throughout this discussion of gaining new experiences, I've omitted seeking a new degree. Although that path may be an option if you have a clear idea of what you want to do next, trying to educate yourself out of a box that education put you into doesn't strike me as a successful strategy. In any case, pursuing law or medicine will require specialized professional guidance that goes beyond the scope of this book.

Making Time for New Activities

"But wait," you may be thinking, "I barely have time for my work as it is. How can I conduct informational interviews *and* throw myself into new activities?" My playful reply is that you're entering your "senior spring" as an academic. More plainly: you have to put scholarly commitments on the back burner in order to build the knowledge and skills that will support a new career.

A common concept in business is the 80–20 rule. This adage states that the first 80 percent of quality comes from the first 20 percent of effort that's theoretically required to complete a project. To move from "good" to "excellent" to "perfect" requires exponentially greater investments of time, money, and work. *If you've already decided to leave academia, it's sufficient to target 80 percent quality—and 20 percent effort—in that sphere.*

Your experience will likely make this shift easier than it seems at first glance. By my last year at Tulane, I'd taught Roman history so often that I could lecture almost without preparation. My study sheets were written, slideshows made, and talking points refined. I could have reread every primary source and fine-tuned my materials—and no doubt would have made the course better by doing so. But as consultants are fond of saying, that juice wasn't worth the squeeze. Consequently, I

simplified my written assignments so they were easier to grade
and lectured from notes without reminding myself of how we
knew each minute detail.

I likewise started to wind down my research. At the time,
I was keeping up with scholarship, tinkering with an article I
wanted to publish, and working on a survey for a future project.
These efforts were essentially habits: the way I turned non-
teaching time into "productive" scholarly outputs. I nevertheless came to see that each minute or hour I gave them prevented
me from working a part-time job, from writing a blog, or from
having an informational interview with someone in a career
I'd overlooked. And while none of them was a major investment on its own, they added up to a significant portion of my
total productivity. Suspending them enabled me to pursue new
experiences that were more helpful to my career change.

When scaling back your academic commitments, avoid
obvious deterioration in your performance. Being absent as a
teacher or lab partner is irresponsible, unethical, and cruel to
your colleagues and students. I'm advising you to do *less*, not
to do *nothing*. When I decided to simplify my Roman history
work, I didn't see any qualitative change in how my students
reacted to lectures or scored on exams. In fact, my evaluations
that semester came back better than ever. I would urge you to
aim for the same balance.

Perhaps you're worried that your college won't appreciate getting just 20 percent of your best effort. Remember
that you don't need to advertise this new disposition—and
that few people should notice any change. The worst possible
outcome is that someone objects and tries to fire you. But so
what? You're already planning to leave the job, and it's unlikely
that they could find someone to replace you midsemester and
on short notice. Compared with the reward you stand to gain

from taking back time from your academic activities, that risk is insignificant.

Development Strategies

Although time will be more plentiful once you pull back from academic efforts, it's not limitless. The speed of your success depends on learning the skills and subject matter that will benefit you most. Consequently, you need to have a game plan when you set out to build experience. Two main approaches are available: focus on a single skill set or pursue more varied learning.

If discovery has taught you without a doubt what you want your new career to be, it's better to be targeted. Build a cluster of skills that you know are essential for the job you want. Even if that means spending all your time learning Excel and Quick-Books, forge ahead. Along with your academic background, those new skills may be enough to get you noticed—or at least to reassure recruiters that you're dedicated to working in their field.

Those of you who still aren't sure what you'd like to do can pursue more diverse experiences. Dipping your toes in lots of streams will let you simultaneously develop a range of skills and figure out a type of work that suits you.

I deployed the latter strategy. After realizing I stacked up poorly against others in the New Orleans market, I said yes to nearly every opportunity that presented itself. I enrolled in night classes, joined the finance committee of a nonprofit, and started a blog. I began working for a friend, then joined the board of another nonprofit. For two weeks, I tutored at an after-school program. I even convened a consortium of Contingent Faculty Committee chairs from other academic disciplines.

All of these activities came on top of teaching three courses at Tulane, running the Contingent Faculty Committee for the Society for Classical Studies, and conducting informational interviews with people around town. And I was actively applying for jobs, too.

It's tiring even to list all of these efforts—and I'll admit I was exhausted while doing them. But together they gave me six new lines on my résumé, each reflecting a new skill or accomplishment. In fact, I gained so much experience in such a short time that I was able to move my visiting assistant professorship to the third position in my résumé's list of past roles. This frenzy of activity also provided a wealth of anecdotes I could use to quell doubts when a hiring manager wasn't sure I could adapt to a new environment.

Moving between different roles at breakneck pace also taught me how to change gears quickly. By the end of this process, I thought nothing of jumping from writing and teaching into taxes and accounts, or from websites and want ads to donors and donuts. Little did I know that such frenetic activity was training me for my future life: my current work rarely affords more than thirty minutes to give a task my undivided attention.

Developing new skills—even on a part-time basis—has another benefit: it puts you into contact with people who spend their days committed to activities you're likely to do in the future. As you get to know these professionals, they cease to appear as aliens living a strange existence. You learn that they're people with strengths and weaknesses like your own, and that most are excited to hear your perspective. This familiarity soon makes you colleagues and friends—and when it does, you stop viewing yourself as an academic intruder in their space. You see yourself as one of them.

This dovetailing of experience and familiarity occurred for me after nearly a year of seizing any opportunity I could to build new skills and knowledge. A company that I'd been following posted an interesting job, and I quickly set to work tweaking my résumé to appear a good fit for their culture. As I reviewed how their employees cast themselves online, a peculiar fact dawned on me: these were the same people I'd been intimidated by when I began looking at nonacademic jobs. I could still recognize a gap between my professional experience and theirs, but it was far less obvious than it had been just twelve months before.

I realized in that moment that I'd successfully forged myself into the type of candidate I'd aimed to become. I'd built a range of skills through work in business and nonprofit settings—and had grown comfortable interacting with the sorts of people I desired as colleagues. From then on, I knew it was safe to narrow my focus. I kept up a few of the activities that I found especially meaningful, but otherwise limited myself to opportunities that could help me secure a career in communications strategy.

Cultivating a Public Persona

To be offered a job, you have to convince an employer that you'll add more value to their organization than they'll pay you for your efforts. This dynamic is true for any business, nonprofit, or government organization. Consequently, your success depends on becoming a "salesperson of yourself."

Some people take a page from the marketing industry and describe this activity as building a personal brand. Whatever you think of that metaphor, the thought behind it isn't bad. It simply means you should present yourself in a catchy and memorable way, and do so consistently in every area you might be seen. In the digital age, there are two main places that can happen: social media and a personal website.

At the risk of stating the obvious, Facebook is for friends. The information there is often personal—and can include photos from younger days when we may have acted less professionally than we would today. Even if you think your profile is innocuous, lock it down. You can prevent employers from seeing what's there by setting your profile to private and only allowing friends of friends to access it. Just in case, untag old pictures where you're passed out in a bar or doing anything illicit. Many of us have a few of *those* moments, but your career search is like a publicity blitz: you want to control what people see.

The same advice goes for Instagram, Twitter, and whatever seventy-three new platforms have come and gone by the time this book goes to print. A good standard to apply is the directive my grad department chair offered to every new cohort of teaching assistants: "Before you say or do anything, ask whether you'd be comfortable with your mother seeing it on the front page of the newspaper tomorrow morning." In the digital age, heeding that advice means setting your social media profiles to "private" and keeping *every* post professional just in case it reaches a wider audience.

LinkedIn is a special case. A useful way to think of your profile on this platform is as a digital introduction to your professional self. You *want* it to be public—and to be as complete as possible. When I revise mine, I try to imagine I'm standing in an interview and need to give the twenty-second version of who I am, how I add value, and what I do. In this regard LinkedIn is similar to the "elevator pitch" you're taught to have for your dissertation: a short, canned version of your professional self that's designed to pique the interest of whoever reads or hears it.

If you haven't signed up for LinkedIn yet, do it today. If you have a profile you're not actively using, set it to public and update what's there. To the greatest extent you can, make this page mirror the information you have on your résumé and update the two of them in tandem as you narrow your job search and refine your self-presentation.

You might also consider building a personal website. Doing so is a low-effort way to demonstrate concern for your professional image. Free services like Squarespace and WordPress look great and don't require any knowledge of HTML (a fear that prevented me from making a site sooner, and that likely shows my age). In just a few hours, you can learn the platform, lay out your site, and write any copy (i.e., text) you want to include.

If you have some money to spare, you can even buy a custom URL. The cost varies by host, but ".com" domains usually run less than $25 per year. It may be vain, but I'm happy to shoulder that expense to tell people they can visit www.christophercaterine .com.

My personal site served multiple purposes as I was changing careers. It hosted the blog I used to practice writing for nonacademic audiences, allowed me to showcase my personal and professional interests, and provided a forum to display my knowledge and accomplishments. Although the site's contents have evolved in the years since I left higher education, it initially featured pages on my personal background, contingent faculty issues, craft beer, and classical studies.

Unless you're seeking work in graphic design, a website is unlikely to be *the* element of your professional persona that convinces someone to interview you. But it can help tip the scales. By presenting yourself consistently across platforms, you inspire confidence that you are who you say you are and that you aren't overly manipulating your application to qualify for a specific job. Likewise, by showcasing your talents in or knowledge of writing, photography, or any other topic, you make it easy for people to learn more about you—and increase the likelihood that they'll want to chat at greater length.

Whatever public forums you decide to occupy, be *assiduously positive*. I know academics often interact through mutual complaints, but the Internet is not the place for that behavior when you're trying to start a new career.

If a potential employer reads a post where you mock a student or lament an injustice you suffered in your job, it's unlikely they'll be sympathetic. Instead, they'll worry you might speak about *them* in the same way. At that point, it makes no difference whether you're justified in what you said: you look like a liability. The hiring manager will move to their next candidate, and you'll remain unemployed.

This advice doesn't mean you can't call people out when they act inappropriately. Rather, it's a reminder that you should be cautious in the criticism you commit to writing and put online for the world to see. You're already at a disadvantage as someone who's changing careers; don't compound the risk by venting into cyberspace. Keep complaints in the safe space of the real world.

Finding Open Positions

It's tempting to treat job applications as a numbers game. While it's true that you want to put as many lines in the water as you can, doing so indiscriminately almost never hooks a fish you want to keep.

Academics make this mistake often—and Vay Cao fell victim to it herself. When she began applying for jobs, she targeted any listing her résumé might plausibly fit. She didn't understand, at least at first, why she didn't get any replies.

Vay is braver than I am: she kept these applications and occasionally goes back to see what she wrote. Doing so has allowed her to realize that she often didn't know how to interpret a job's requirements. You might think, for example, that as a teacher you're an obvious fit for a nonprofit seeking someone with "great communication skills." But unless you know what that phrase means in the context of that organization, you're likely to miss the mark when enumerating your specific talents.

Consequently, many academics apply to jobs they're completely unqualified for without ever knowing it. As Vay learned the hard way, that ignorance makes it easy to waste a lot of time. The good news is that if you've conducted discovery in the ways I recommended earlier, you should be in a better position to avoid this pitfall.

When it comes to finding open positions, there are multiple resources you can use. I've already mentioned LinkedIn. This platform is increasingly where employers post jobs first, so you'll want to check it regularly. You can filter open positions by title, skill, salary, location, and a range of other criteria. Just remember to keep your profile up to date: some listings will allow you to apply through the platform by sending recruiters a link to your public LinkedIn page.

Most organizations also have a section on their website dedicated to open jobs. If you know you want to work for a specific company, nonprofit, or government office, check their listings every month. If that page is the sole place where the organization lists jobs, do so every week. Outside of academia, many jobs get filled when the hiring manager identifies a viable candidate—not after a fixed application period has elapsed.

There are also larger job board sites such as Indeed.com and Monster.com (two of the most popular in the United States at the time of writing). Like LinkedIn, they offer a wide range of search criteria to find positions that match your wants and needs, and in some cases let you apply directly through the site. Unfortunately, few academics secure interviews in this way. These sites automatically screen applicants for specific skills and experience, so your résumé might never pass in front of a real person. I would still check them periodically to look for "ideal fit" positions, but otherwise you should treat them as a way to identify suitable job titles and assemble lists of skills required for positions you want (as discussed in the "Discover" chapter).

Local job sites are often better—and somewhere I personally had greater luck. The organizations that use them to fill open positions are normally smaller and less rigid in their thinking about what constitutes a relevant professional background. They also tend to have a stated mission of hiring people from the local community, which is helpful if you're already living where you want to work.

You can also attend job fairs at the college that employs you or participate in networking events hosted by schools you've attended. Meeting people in these contexts allows you to bypass the virtual gate checks that can keep nontraditional applicants from advancing: you'll hand your résumé directly to a recruiter who can get it where it needs to go. Just make sure you have your pitch down. Since you'll be an unusual participant, you need to be clear about the value you can add to attending organizations—and pose smart questions about the jobs they're filling.

Certain programs also exist specifically to draw people with advanced degrees into critical areas. The American Presidential Management Fellowship, for example, connects recent master's and doctoral graduates to job openings in executive branch agencies. Many government offices likewise have internal initiatives to train smart people to do essential jobs. The FBI considers PhDs for their special agent program, provided you can meet the physical requirements of the job. A friend who applied with the Bureau reports that they were the *only* employer he met with who didn't question the benefit of his humanities doctorate. That incident wasn't isolated: while serving as a character reference for another friend's security clearance, an agent similarly urged me to put my intellect into the service of my country.

A final way to find a new position is through a headhunter. Companies hire these professionals to fill roles with capable and qualified talent that they intend to keep for an extended time. There's really no risk to you in this arrangement: the headhunter's fee is calculated as a percentage of the salary you're offered—but the company has to pay it. While I don't know of any academics who were successful with this approach, absolutely proceed if you find a headhunter who's excited about your story and wants to shop your résumé around.

Don't pick and choose between the approaches I've just described: attempt as many as you can. Apply to at least a few positions each week, and feel free to seek multiple roles at the same organization. Few managers will notice that you've applied for more than one job, and those that do may be intrigued by your tenacity. On one occasion, a CEO interviewed me for a position he knew I couldn't fill because my name had crossed his desk a few times in quick succession.

And when you *are* called in for a meeting, always say yes. Even if you think you don't want the job, you'll benefit from the practice—and might change your mind after meeting the team and learning more about the opportunity.

Connecting to the Right Opportunities

Some people advise those leaving academia to focus on smaller firms. These entities erect fewer barriers between applicants and the people who can hire them, making it easier to ford what I call the "corporate moat." An organization of thirty people is unlikely to have robots sending your résumé to the trash, and the manager who screens your file in the morning might spend the afternoon doing client work with the CEO. If an aspect of your résumé stands out—a doctorate, say, or your experience as a professor—curiosity alone might convince them to call you in.

Inversely, it might be harder to get your foot in the door at large organizations, but they're more capable of absorbing the cost and risk of bringing you on board. Global consultancies demonstrate this principle well. Their colossal size means that they don't feel the six or so months that it often takes new hires to carry their own weight: that burden gets spread out over *hundreds of thousands* of other professionals.[2] Likewise, they have established training programs that prepare you to do your new job without overburdening your colleagues. The probability of securing a position at one of these organizations—or

2. This number isn't an exaggeration. In 2019, leading consultancies reported the following global head counts: Accenture: 459,000; IBM: 378,000; Deloitte: 312,000; Cognizant: 281,000; Ernst & Young (EY): 270,000; PricewaterhouseCoopers (PwC): 251,000; Capgemini: 211,000.

any entity that employs more than a few hundred people—is consequently higher once you've begun the interview process. Experience has taught me that there's truth in both these philosophies. When I tried to get the attention of boutique firms, I secured a good number of meetings. But it was ultimately a global company that made me an offer.

Wherever you find an open position, take special care if the job is an especially good fit for your skills, interests, and background. Tailor the summary section of your résumé to the role and use the body of that document to flag the skills they're seeking in the job listing. If they want you to submit your résumé by email, send it with a brief message that summarizes why you're a good fit. Just remember: nobody assumes you can add value to their organization. It's your job to convince them that it's in *their* interests to speak with you at greater length.

Your résumé and transmittal email don't need to be the last word on the subject. If a friend or contact works at the organization, ask them to mention your name to the person in charge of hiring. You don't need to say anything more than that. The hardest part of getting an interview is getting your application noticed, and simply hearing your name may be enough to make that happen. Of course, it helps if your contact can put in a good word on your behalf, but leave that matter to their discretion: they know the organization's culture and people far better than you, and they'll be more likely to help if you're tactful when asking them for assistance.

If you don't know a current employee, you can try to get yourself noticed through a second-degree connection. Search LinkedIn for a contact who knows someone at the organization where you're applying, then ask for an introduction. When doing so, be careful to ask only for an *informational interview*. Treat the call as a chance to learn about the organization's culture and dynamics as someone who's considering an open job there. If the discussion goes well—and the other person is willing and empowered to speak on your behalf—they'll likely say so by the end of the call.

You can also try to contact a hiring manager directly by calling or showing up in person. Doing so will demonstrate your interest in a job—and certainly make you stand out in a culture where so much recruitment is managed online. As discussed earlier, this approach helped Michael Zimm get an interview with a small digital marketing firm in his home city. Just be careful to read the situation: if you get the sense a company or individual recruiter isn't open to direct contact, back off immediately.

One final piece of advice on this topic: remember to continue networking as you apply for positions. Research conducted by Lou Adler has shown that 85 percent of all jobs are filled via referral, and his estimates suggest that employers are seven times more likely to notice you if you're actively sustaining relationships while you seek work.[3]

Planning for the End of the Race

As you apply for jobs that will mark the start your new career, you also should pause to consider how you'll respond when an offer finally comes. There are numerous reasons why such an assessment is useful. First, you won't necessarily *want* the first position you get. Understanding how much flexibility your personal circumstances allow will enable you to make an informed

---

3. Lou Adler, "New Study Reveals 85% of All Jobs Are Filled via Networking," *LinkedInPulse*, February 29, 2016: https://www.linkedin.com/pulse/new-survey-reveals-85-all-jobs-filled-via-networking-lou-adler.

decision that's right for you. Second, a good opportunity may come at a bad time—and you may be forced to make a difficult choice.

If you're at a point where you have to accept any position you're offered, that's perfectly fine. Nothing says you have to hold that job forever. My advice throughout this book is meant to guide you to a satisfying *career*, not just a new role. Approach positions that seem bad as "starter jobs" and use them to build new skills until you're qualified for better opportunities. Just make sure you keep networking and applying so you don't get mired in a position you hate.

If you have the freedom to wait for an offer you really like, now is a good time to review the values you prioritized during discernment and make sure your career search is still aligned with your goals. Set limits on how long you can afford to put off starting a new position—especially if you decide to do so while unemployed. "Afford" doesn't just mean support financially: equally important are your personal sanity and how a lengthy gap on a former academic's résumé will look to hiring managers.

For me, the challenge at this stage was preventing my love of New Orleans from threatening my financial stability. The job market in this city is notoriously limited, and in the middle of my job search a local paper even ran a feature on young professionals leaving for better opportunities. Knowing this risk, my wife and I set a deadline: if I was unable to find work within six months of my last paycheck, I'd expand my search to other regions. We didn't want to leave the city, but we knew that relying on one salary wasn't sustainable.

If you're seeking jobs while still active in academia, it's also possible you'll get an offer in the middle of the semester. Should this event occur, you'll face a tricky ethical dilemma: accept the new job straightaway or finish teaching? Making this call isn't easy. On the one hand, you have to consider the work you've invested to find a new career and the prospects the offer affords you. On the other, you may worry about those who would be harmed by a decision to leave abruptly: your students, colleagues, or lab team.

The best-case scenario is that you negotiate with your new employer to begin the position after the academic term. Yes, you get to negotiate. And yes, the date you begin work is a common point in those discussions. Some employers may even appreciate your desire for a delay: if you give your current boss the courtesy of finishing projects you've committed to, your new one may infer that you'd do the same for them. Just don't use all your leverage to help your school without getting something extra for yourself. Yes, you can and should negotiate on salary, too.

You may wish to negotiate more aggressively on a start date if leaving academia unexpectedly would have an outsized impact on other people. For example, you might have lab mates or research partners whose own professional success depends on your continued efforts, or your college might serve large populations of first-generation or low-income students. In these situations, do everything in your power to be fair to all parties—and let your own sense of morality guide your final decision.

Unfortunately, a job offer may only be valid if you start immediately, forcing you to quit on short notice or let the opportunity pass. In this position, I would strongly urge you to accept the job and let your department or college manage the fallout. Although my advice on this point is unorthodox (and my editor and reviewers ask that you take it with a grain of salt), I've come to believe that quitting a job midsemester is the only way to change the incentive structures that make work in the modern academy so challenging.

There are numerous reasons I think such a decision is appropriate, even if it throws your colleagues and students under the proverbial bus.

First, your primary concern in any contract negotiation needs to be your own success and happiness. You've been working towards this moment for months, and you shouldn't give up an opportunity to work for an employer who's excited to have you out of a sense of obligation to one who isn't.

Second, for all that you're acculturated to believe you must teach through the end of the semester, you may not be under any obligation to do so. I reviewed my contract and administrative policies at length. Both were silent on this matter. The reason wasn't too hard to figure out: I live in a right-to-work state that allows either party to sever an employment relationship at any time for any reason. This dynamic led to a peculiar fact: my contract set a clear timeline for me to teach, but didn't establish any mechanism to prevent me from quitting. If you find yourself in the same situation (and about half of my US readers will), you may be able to leave a teaching job without serious repercussions. Just be sure to read your contract carefully and consult with your college ombudsperson or a legal expert before acting.

The last reason you should leave is to my mind the most important: if a college wants the security of locking you into your position through the end of the term, they should damn well pay for the privilege. Every other sector uses compensation to retain good talent. Colleges and universities, meanwhile, abuse your passion, goodwill, and dedication to obtain the same end at a fraction of the cost. Most US institutions of higher learning charge students about *ten times* what they pay you. Comparison makes it clear how absurd this situation is: in professions like accounting, law, and consulting, it's seen as fantastic to bill at a multiplier of four.

Colleges get away with this behavior because few of their employees are ever in a position to make them regret it. The entire professoriate has suffered and continues to suffer as a result. Indeed, salaries for this group have remained stagnant while other professionals, including academic administrators, have made significant gains. If you want to do a favor for the academics you leave behind, let your college know the consequence for failing to treat you fairly: the inconvenience of having to fill a teaching gap midsemester—and the wrath of the undergraduates (and their parents) whose courses and course credit will disappear if the school doesn't act.

While this advice may not be popular in some circles, attempts to correct the gross imbalance afflicting the academic labor market have thus far failed. I believe it's now warranted to apply a different sort of pressure. Quitting an academic job in the middle of the semester will convey that you're frustrated with the "adjunctification" of higher education and ready to opt out of that system rather than perpetuate it. Such a statement, made a sufficient number of times, may even elicit a response from college deans, presidents, or boards—and perhaps finally compel more equitable treatment of your academic colleagues and friends.

Should you have to make this decision yourself, know that the dilemma isn't merely theoretical. In 2019, a friend of mine faced it—and opted to accept a new position. The concerns outlined above weighed on him heavily as he confronted the colleagues and students whose lives became more difficult because of his departure. Even so, he's convinced he made the right choice and has allowed me to share his advice to those of you who end up in the same position.

First, consult your college's ombudsperson. These individuals are designated experts in personnel matters, and any conversation with them is normally confidential. They can help you figure out what you're entitled to do, as well as the administrative procedures you need to follow when leaving a position before your contract ends.

Second, be honest but brief. You should only inform your chair that you're leaving after you've signed the contract for your new position. When you have that conversation, be firm on your departure date without getting into details about why you're quitting. If necessary, pivot to explaining the processes you'll need to follow as you transition out of your role: few chairs will have encountered this situation before, and having that information on hand saves them a call to the ombudsperson.

Third, know that it's going to hurt. There's no joy in making life harder for your colleagues, but it's ultimately the department's job to manage any pain that results from your departure. If you're able (and willing) to make the situation easier by recommending a professor to replace you or handing over your course materials, by all means offer that assistance.

Lastly, think about what your students may want to know. Few will understand the complex dynamics of the academic job market. Be prepared to answer why you're leaving a job you're so good at—and convey to them clearly that your departure isn't about them. When my friend informed his students that he was quitting, he felt like a parent telling the children about a divorce. His students were similarly hurt. They craved reassurance. Some cried.

Despite the difficulty of these professional interactions, my friend is certain that it was right for him to leave his position midsemester. Academic culture may discourage using at-will employment to your advantage, but the business model of higher education is cold and transactional. His school never offered him a permanent job, and on multiple occasions they cancelled one of his classes on short notice—then prorated his salary. When faced with the choice of remaining loyal to them or embracing a new opportunity, there was never any real question about what he would do.

Conclusion

The main takeaway of this chapter—and really of this entire book—is that you make your own luck. While it's true that you're more likely to land a job if you increase your number of applications, your odds don't improve in a linear fashion. You'll stand a much better chance of grabbing a manager's attention if you know what type of position you want, shape your résumé to match it, and make your name stand out from other applicants.

At this point you may be wondering how this chapter can end before I've told you how to succeed in a job *interview*. In fact, I don't have substantive advice to add on that topic. Months of informational meetings, résumé creation, and new experiences have prepared you for that opportunity. You know to research whoever you're meeting to get a sense of how they think, to cast your experience in relatable terms, and to explain how your skills (whether old or new) can add value to the organization you'd like to join.

Enter your interviews confidently, trusting that they'll feel like the conversations you're already used to having. Few will be an inquisition. If you're a good candidate for the job, your anecdotes will feed the discussion as you build rapport with the hiring manager. Soon enough, you'll find yourself getting more excited as you speak about work you know you can do—and a second career you won't have to abandon.

Action Items

1. Using your informational interviews as a guide, identify three specific roles you'd be interested in holding. Use LinkedIn and company websites to determine the skills and knowledge you would need to be considered for those jobs.

2. Research and identify three local charities or nonacademic initiatives at your college that you'd be interested in supporting. Send a short note to each to see if they can staff you in a role that would build one of the skills you identified in item 1.

3. Check the privacy settings on your social media accounts and update your public profiles. If you have a personal website, check that its design is clean, that its copy is error-free, and that its pages reflect your new professional persona.

6

Deploy

More than two years after beginning my search for a new career, my wife and I were out to lunch celebrating our wedding anniversary. The restaurant was nice and the food was good, but I'd been on edge for a while.

Three weeks earlier I was in the running for four different jobs. One promised a second interview, but never called back. Another decided to hire someone else. I thought the third was going well, but my contact there had gone silent for more than a week. It seemed like opportunities were evaporating all around me. Even so, I had a good feeling about the last position: I knew the hiring manager from an informational interview, my mix of academic and nonacademic experience was a natural fit for the role, and I'd stayed relaxed and confident throughout my in-person interview.

We'd just been served dessert when my phone rang. Despite the occasion, I left my wife at the table and hurried outside to take the call. I was certain that my wait for a new job was over. But the voice on the other end was cagey. After two awkward minutes, he finally came clean: they had extended an offer to somebody else.

The look on my face conveyed the news as I rejoined my wife in the dining room. We finished our dessert, settled the bill, and left in silence. I could feel my anxiety mount once we were in the car. My heart was pounding, eyes darting, speech erratic. When we finally parked, my wife told me it was time to rip the Band-Aid on the last opportunity. I recall her sitting patiently while I pecked an email into my phone—then biting her tongue as I needlessly tweaked the message for five more minutes:

> I'm sure you're busy with the holiday coming up, but since it's been a week I wanted to check in to see whether you've come to a decision about the position yet. No worries if not—I just don't want to fall through the cracks when people scatter for the Fourth. Best, Chris.

Satisfied but shaking, I pressed "send." One way or another, I'd soon learn my fate. The reply came less than a minute later:

> Gave the green light to Talent so you should hear back soon after the fourth. Have a wonderful weekend.

As the meaning of those nineteen words sunk in, my jaw dropped: I was no longer an academic.

Preparing for Change

The elation of getting your first nonacademic job offer is incomparable. Take a moment to celebrate, but know that in its wake come three new and daunting questions:

1. Can I actually do the job I've just accepted?
2. What habits do I need to develop or jettison to be successful?

3. How can I acclimate to my new environment as quickly as possible?

Having doubt in each of these areas is normal when you're leaving academia. The truth is that you don't *really* know what work will be like in your new profession—and odds are you won't get much time to relax before you're put to the test.

Let me offer a few words to put your mind at ease. First, your new organization's success now depends on yours. Unless the people you're working with are astonishingly inept, they won't just throw you into the deep end to see whether you can swim: they'll train you in your new responsibilities and do everything they can to ease your transition into the role. Anyone tasked with your orientation will also know that your background is untraditional—and will expect your knowledge of your new job to be uneven.

Second, you likely have more transferable skills than you realize. As discussed in other chapters, your academic work was extremely varied. Each day you had to research, synthesize and present data, and tailor messages to diverse audiences. At turns you played disciplinarian and offered sympathy, watched for psychological distress and found ways to challenge students who were ready to excel. Years spent moving between these diverse roles has made you a confident actor in unfamiliar contexts—and a quick study in what's required to succeed. Your past experience will assist you in a thousand ways you don't expect once you actually get to work.

Third, nobody will trust you with a job unless they're confident you can perform at the level required. Pity hires don't exist—if only because managers get blamed when subordinates fail. So put that fear aside. For all that you may feel in over your head, others will see you as a bright and eager new employee who brings a fresh perspective. And like any new employee, they'll expect you to make mistakes.

Making Mistakes: A Case Study

About ten months into my current job, I had a chance to impress someone I'd been waiting to meet for more than a year. The director in question had agreed to an informational interview the prior spring, and afterwards had passed my résumé to a colleague who was hiring. He was *the person* who got me noticed and helped me leave academia. I didn't want to disappoint him, and confidence in how quickly I'd adapted to my role inspired me to swing for the fences.

There's that word again. Confidence. When presenting a big idea I'd been asked to develop, I completely missed the mark: my pitch fell flat with the senior people in the room, the person I'd hoped to dazzle took over that part of my work, and I got saddled with less important tasks for the duration of the project.

This outcome was clearly *not* what I'd hoped for. I was disappointed in myself, but even more embarrassed that I'd failed so spectacularly in front of someone whose trust I wanted to earn. A few weeks later, though, we had a chance to talk it over. The director shrugged off my failure and assured me that it's normal to make rookie mistakes in your rookie year. If I committed a similar error in eighteen months, we'd need to have a different chat. For now, he was content to treat it as a learning experience.

After a moment he even started to chuckle. He said he'd also tried to wow people he admired when he started at the firm, and that it was amusing to inspire that emotion in someone else. In the end, he not only put my worries at ease, but found a way to turn my discomfort into a source of connection.

Overcoming Culture Shock

It's good to know that a few mistakes—even embarrassing ones—won't spell disaster in a new job. Still, you don't want to make them a habit. Avoiding faux pas is ultimately about understanding the dynamics of your environment, particularly as they relate to human interactions. The challenge for academics is that the world you're entering can seem utterly foreign when you arrive.

Every organization has its own culture and vernacular. Even if you've conducted informational interviews diligently over the last few months, your new colleagues will talk differently, carry themselves differently, even interact differently than you're used to. Functioning as a full and equal member of this new ecosystem requires you to learn from them and adapt your behavior accordingly.

Let's start with language. Many of the words people use will sound as foreign to you as Navajo, Greek, or the jargon of literary theory do to nonexperts. If you're in an organization that deals with technology and software development, your colleagues may obsess about scrums and stacks, use "agile" as a noun, or fret over service metrics and deliverables. Other sectors will have their own lexical tics. If you find yourself at a loss, just remind the person speaking that you don't have a technical background and ask for an explanation in lay terms.

Regardless of sector, you're likely to hear a plethora of abstract nouns and verbs (think: *-ation* and *-ize* words). People often pile these terms atop one another because they think using "big words" makes them sound intelligent. This habit leads to awkward, dense formulations like "It's necessary that we optimize our sales deck by leveraging strategic learnings from past implementations." Such expressions may seem unintelligible (to say nothing of infelicitous as specimens of the English language), but they convey real sense within groups that are used to communicating in this manner. While you don't have to speak this way yourself, do learn to keep up when others do so.

You may also see people smash words together and violate every orthographic standard your teachers drilled into you. "Simultaneous software development and IT operations" doesn't sound very cool, so tech folks call it DevOps. The company Accenture got its name because they put the *accent* on the *future*. Vowel dropping and alternative spellings apparently strike marketers as futuristic (e.g., Tumblr, Scribd, BHLDN). The variety is truly endless, and people beyond academia seem to have as much fun penning portmanteaux as a gossip columnist does naming celebrity couples.

Leaving academia also means learning new acronyms and initialisms. Although you might *think* you already have it bad on this front, letters masquerading as words fly even more freely in other professional contexts. RACI matrixes, KPIs, SOWs, and NDAs are just the beginning.[1] Every industry has its own way of abbreviating ubiquitous concepts, and learning them necessarily takes time and repeated exposure. If you're worried that you'll slow down conversation by constantly asking

---

1. For the uninitiated, these abbreviations stand for "responsible, accountable, consulted, informed" (describing the level of involvement different stakeholders have in a detailed matrix of tasks that make up a larger project), "key performance indicators," "statements of work," and "nondisclosure agreements."

what terms mean, remember that most abbreviations come up quickly when you plug them into a search engine next to the name of your industry.

Not every difference in language is confusing, even if much of it is new. Two and a half years out of academia, I'm still surprised at how pervasive emoji are in professional correspondence—and it's a rare day in my job when I *don't* have occasion to use one.

Patricia Soler understands how differences in verbiage and modes of discourse can leave you feeling dizzy. During her time as a scholar of Latin American studies, she spoke, thought, and wrote exclusively in Spanish and Portuguese. In fact, her job at the US Department of Housing and Urban Development (HUD) was the first professional experience she had communicating in her native tongue. But the English at her new job didn't sound like anything she'd heard before. As a result, she sometimes felt slow on the uptake or missed the point of discussions—precisely what you *don't* want to do when starting a position.

Patricia was experiencing culture shock within her own country, and the learning curve she faced was as steep as it was unexpected. But steep isn't insurmountable, especially for someone with so much practice learning. Over time, Patricia picked up on the terms people used most often and discerned their meaning through context or by asking. Before she knew it, she was fluent in the office lingo.

After clearing that initial hurdle, Patricia began to stand out from her peers. Soon she was recommended for new roles—and even received an offer to lead a different team at HUD. That experience subsequently helped her change careers for the *second* time: she recently left her role as a program analyst to become an IT specialist.

In addition to learning a new language, you'll also have to adapt to the unspoken rules and modes of interaction that shape behavior at your office. Some organizations are formal and hierarchical, while others aspire to be more egalitarian. In fact, there are as many cultures as there are government agencies, businesses, and nonprofits—each one with an array of dynamics that influence how people dress, how junior and senior staff speak to one another, how decisions get made and communicated, and infinite other subtleties of how work gets done. Adapting your behavior to these norms will make you part of the team faster and convince any doubters that you were indeed a good hire.

Your interview will give you some indication of these invisible forces, but you only learn how people *really* interact once you're on the job. To acculturate faster, start by observing more than you speak. Until you understand what your job requires and how personal dynamics influence particular situations, it's easy to misread a room. Your new colleagues will forgive some errors of this type during your first months on the job, but limiting them will help you earn trust and respect as quickly as possible.

Small talk requires special care. When one of your new colleagues opens up, it will be tempting for you to do the same. If the discussion is about sports or family, you're surely safe. But exercise caution if there's even a hint of complaining about coworkers, clients, or the organization itself. Until you understand the political dynamics at your office—which may take eighteen months or more—staying positive is your safest course of action. Doing so will protect you from being known as a complainer and avoid a situation where a comment made out of ignorance gets back to the wrong person.

Being guarded doesn't mean you should isolate yourself. Solicit advice from as many people as you can and try to interact with coworkers in job functions different from your own. It's easy to be drawn in by the first person to take you under their wing, but even someone with good intentions only offers one perspective. To thrive in your new environment, it's best to pull information from many sources and to form as complete an understanding as possible of the organization and its culture.

One trick is to make sure you ask the right person the right question. A chief executive officer (CEO) or executive director (XD, the nonprofit equivalent of a CEO) isn't going to have time to tell you about logging hours, though she may be thrilled to let her new hire know how she's positioning the organization in the market. Conversely, a secretary most likely won't understand the nuances of a fiscal strategy, but he can probably tell you more than anybody else about the organization's structure and how people interact within the office. Your first days in a job are often likened to drinking from a firehose. Amid that flood, make a special effort to remember who knows what so you can solicit information more effectively in the future.

Also respect people's time when you consider asking for help. Answers to "who," "what," or "where" questions are often available on your organization's intranet or in its written policies. Look that information up yourself. In situations where you'd like to know how or why something is done, you'll usually find colleagues are happy to share their perspectives. Just make sure you address your question to the most appropriate person—and ask them to redirect you if there's a better source.

If this advice sounds obvious, it's because acculturating yourself to a professional environment isn't terribly different from academic research. Your first few months in a job are a chance to observe the organization, assess its operations, synthesize your findings, and develop hypotheses for further consideration and testing. The difference is that you're now in the thick of the action: your calculations can have real and immediate consequences.

David Stevens navigated this strait skillfully. After leaving Princeton as an ABD ("all but dissertation") in political science, his work with a think tank in New York gave him dual responsibilities: tutoring business professionals in international politics and participating in conferences of policymakers and journalists. David consequently had to learn not just the culture of his employer, but also the languages, thought processes, and dynamics of the three new fields he interacted with.

No matter how much David imitated these groups, they always read his comportment as academic. Ironically, this occurred for different reasons: the journalists noticed that he focused on long narratives instead of short stories with an immediate impact, while policy professionals thought he applied theory to issues more than "real-life" practitioners. His viewpoints were thus distinctive—and consistently made him stand out.

David turned this combination of cultural knowledge and imperfect adaptation to his advantage. Quite uniquely, he can "go deep" while talking to experts in each of the communities he interacts with *and* translate their concerns into terms that professionals in the other areas will understand. Today, he's found success using his position as an outsider with insider knowledge to challenge people's assumptions and help them see beyond their myopia—a skill fueled by his curiosity in understanding how different fields think, speak, and behave.

Building New Relationships

I initially thought that *efficiency* would be the prime measure of success in my current job—and that consultants would avoid small talk to get down to business. This assumption made intuitive sense from the outside: in my line of work, the stakes are high, the compensation generous, and the people driven to succeed. I couldn't imagine why anyone would care how I spent my weekend. As I quickly learned, though, good relationships are essential for professionals to work together. A strong rapport catalyzes everything from emails to strategic planning. Ironically, small talk can produce efficiency.

Unless it's 7:00 p.m. the night before a deadline or senior leaders make it clear they're not in the mood to chat, you'll be well served by taking a few minutes to banter. Ask people how their kids are doing, whether they hit the same traffic as you on the way in, what they have planned for the next holiday, anything. Opening up the room and acknowledging the people around you *as people* will build empathy and trust, two assets you can never have enough of.

The reason why is easy to see. At some point, every team faces an unexpected challenge like lost funding or a missed deadline. When that happens, nobody will be at their best. You'll have to work late nights, shoulder new responsibilities, and do whatever it takes to right the ship. It's amazing in those moments how a joke built on some little detail you picked up earlier can break the tension and keep everyone in the room from going crazy.

The good news is that building rapport should be second nature to you after years of teaching and months of informational interviews. You're highly practiced in meeting people one-on-one or in group settings, in reading the energy they bring to a discussion, and in adjusting as needed to connect with them effectively. These skills will come out naturally when you interact with others in your workplace. Just remember to prime the relationship by applying the techniques I've described throughout this book: prepare a succinct "elevator pitch" about your role, ask more questions than you answer, and mind your interlocutor's tone and body language so they can guide the conversation.

Getting Down to Business (or Government or Nonprofit)

When other people make it clear they're ready to work, get to the point. Focus on details that are relevant to your audience, particularly in emails. It's best practice to flag what you want, who's involved, and when you need it within the first two lines. Don't worry about seeming rude. Stating critical information up front is actually *polite*, as it saves your readers time and decreases the odds that they will miss your request. Few people read past a subject and snippet unless it's clear they have a pressing reason to continue.

Also avoid the temptation to explain every request. Few people care *why* work demands their attention: they just want to know what they're required to do. A lengthy treatment of the decision process that led to your request only opens the door to second-guessing. Anybody who wants additional insight will ask for further information.

For me, economy of speech has been an ongoing battle. Academia trains you to read the entire body of scholarship relevant to a topic, to enumerate every issue you can identify with past approaches, and only then to recommend an alternative or state your conclusion. This spadework is the basis of your authority on a subject—at least until you reach a senior level and your opinion carries weight on its own. After so many years of practice, it's hard to break this reflex.

But remember that outside academia, practical results matter above almost all else. In a dynamic marketplace, you can never study every detail or obtain absolute certainty about a course of action. Informed decisions are defined as those that are most probable based on available information, and people simply have to trust one another to provide realistic assessments. Fortunately, everyone knows that deadlines limit how much ground you can cover. As long as you've focused on the highest priority issues and done your best to understand or tackle them, speak with authority and move on to your next task.

Growing as You Go

It's also helpful to solicit feedback from supervisors or colleagues after every project, deadline, or other milestone you complete. Learning where you excel and where you have room to grow is the only way to get better at your job. Seek guidance humbly, listen intently, and take practical steps to apply the advice you receive.

After all the years you spent as a scholar, this exercise should be easy. Academics subject themselves to scathing feedback all the time: grad school is itself a gauntlet, and matters only get worse when you submit papers and books for double-blind review. We all have stories of criticism being leveled at our work—especially *negative* criticism, and all too often *unreasonable* criticism. Like every successful academic, you're practiced in sifting constructive advice from less helpful attacks to create a better final product.

Some of you may be thinking: "Being used to criticism doesn't mean I want to *ask* for it." Fair enough. But remember that you're seeking a face-to-face chat with someone you work with on a daily basis, not a double-blind review. The experience will likely be easier than you expect. In fact, people outside of academia are generally polite—and managers are trained to deliver two pieces of positive feedback for every issue they raise.

Soliciting criticism will also make you stand out. In non-academic settings, it's rare for someone to ask what they did *wrong*. Many have fragile egos and do whatever they can to avoid looking like they made a mistake. Being proactive and showing a desire to learn will differentiate you from those peers. Moreover, it may impress superiors who are eager to reward employees that take their performance seriously.

Some caution is required, though, when it comes to *sharing* criticism. One day it will be your turn to give a colleague feedback or publicly react to an idea in the middle of a meeting. Set alarms to go off in your head when these scenarios occur. Academia has trained you to assess ideas quickly and to nip bad ones in the bud. This reflex serves a good intellectual purpose, but an office isn't an intellectual environment: it's a *political one*.

Generally speaking, the world beyond academia has less tolerance for deconstructing bad ideas. You should still point out when a group is diving down a rabbit hole or pursuing a risky solution, but you need to do so in a manner that is both constructive and kind. When suggesting that someone else's idea won't work, be ready with a viable alternative or at least a path to arrive at one. Likewise, don't deliver your criticism in a way that creates public shame. Doing so will make it harder to work with that colleague in the future and could even lead people to reject your good idea if they think you delivered it with malice.

Discussing Your Past

In the midst of so many new concerns, you'll likely wonder whether or when to reveal your academic past to clients and coworkers. Unless you're in an industry that's adjacent to higher education or get brought into a small company as "the resident professor," most of the former academics I've spoken with advise remaining quiet about your PhD as long as possible. That guidance means keeping it off your email signature and business cards—and perhaps off your name and headline on LinkedIn.

There are numerous reasons for this advice. Some people may see a decision to trumpet an advanced degree as arrogance—a way to belittle people with less education. This interpretation is most likely to occur in sectors like government or manufacturing where seniority traditionally drove promotion and leaders may have come up at a time when a high school diploma was the only qualification required. Whatever pride you (rightly) have in your achievement isn't worth the risk of offending your new peers or superiors.

The tech industry poses a different set of challenges. This sector sees itself as radically democratic and egalitarian—and people care more about what you're *doing* than what you *learned* to earn a degree. A doctorate may be perceived as irrelevant in that context, and some may even view it as an attempt to paper over lack of substance.

Regardless of sector, you'll also encounter people who are suspicious of academia. Maybe they consider it too theoretical, see it as a bad investment, or distrust it for political reasons. Whatever the cause, keeping quiet about your past will buy you time to prove your abilities to these individuals. Once you've built sufficient trust and rapport, you can introduce the information on your own terms and in a way that makes you look interesting instead of underqualified.

Seven months into my current job, I was able to disclose my academic training in a way that felt scripted. I'd just been staffed on a new project with a team that had worked together before. Initially, I kept quiet. I only asked questions when I needed clarification, and while I didn't avoid conversation, I didn't volunteer many personal details about myself, either.

While biding my time, I studied how the team interacted. The senior partner kept the atmosphere in the conference room light, shooting playful barbs at people he knew well and laughing when he got them back in turn. It helped that everyone did their part to keep the work on track: within two weeks, we were ahead of schedule.

One day, during a document review, someone asked about the *lorem ipsum* filler text that stood in an incomplete part of a slideshow. The group began to joke about writing the content in Latin. When the head partner said he'd taken the language in high school and might try it for fun, I saw my opening: "If you're serious, I can work it up in a few hours." Perplexed, he asked me to explain. That's when I finally let them know about my past: my last job had been teaching Latin literature and Roman history.

The team got a laugh out of this exchange and was excited to make sense of why I approached my work differently from other consultants. Soon, writing in Latin became a running gag between me and the rest of the group. I knew in that moment that I was truly one of them—and that I wasn't just faking my way through my new career.

Maintaining Old Relationships

Becoming comfortable in your new identity is a great feeling, but it carries one final challenge you'll have to confront as a former academic: how to maintain ties to your old life.

Depending on your personality, experience, and long-term goals, you'll no doubt have different answers to this question.

Some of you will want to break completely with your academic past. As long as you can account for the time you spent on your degree, this approach may work for you—and even make it easier to adapt to your new life. I personally wouldn't go that route, but I know (or rather knew) one person who did. As far as I can tell from LinkedIn, he's happy and successful.

If you retain bonds of affection for your discipline, the challenge is figuring out the right type and balance of activities for the life you want to lead. Perhaps you'll attend conferences and write articles, or maybe you'll seek new methods of engagement like running blogs, teaching night classes, or even leading book clubs focused on your area of expertise.

Sometimes the line between old and new is fuzzy. During Laura Ansley's time as a grad student at William & Mary, she joined the history blog *Nursing Clio* as a writer and editor. This effort started as a side project, but tracking emails, sending reminders, and keeping people to deadlines made her an excellent project manager. That experience was critical for landing her first postacademic role, as a production editor for the American Society of Civil Engineers.

Nursing Clio has remained a significant part of Laura's life. She was instrumental in the blog's growth over the last four years and now oversees a team of sixteen people as its managing editor. In short, it didn't just enable her to leave academia, it keeps her tethered to an aspect of her discipline that she's eager to continue fostering.

At least for me, it's been possible to derive more joy from my academic area of expertise as a civilian than it was as a professional scholar. Today, I only have to keep up with those aspects of the ancient world that I find fun and meaningful. I can laugh at the jokes in Latin poetry without overthinking them and can use anecdotes from Roman history to demonstrate a point without getting hung up on *Quellenforschung* (source criticism). In fact, I'm happy to report that I haven't muddled through a word of German scholarship in more than four years.

Reaping the Rewards

But what about the benefits of life on the other side? As I said at the start of this book, everyone who's changing careers should figure out what their *life* goals are and pursue a job that enables them. Depending on what you choose to prioritize, you may arrive at an ideal outcome—or you might not. Luck always plays a role.

That said, the vast majority of people who seek employment beyond academia are happy with the decision.[2] Many describe relief at not having to move every summer, having stable health insurance, and earning a salary that covers expenses *and* lets them save. Landing a nonacademic job meant my wife and I could start a family. It gave Mike Zimm a chance to accelerate his career progression by building a marketing department from the ground up less than three years after he left history behind. Kristi Lodge gets to help other people find satisfying careers—not only as an advisor for the University of Oregon's Lundquist College of Business, but also through a company she founded to help humanities PhDs navigate the uncertainty of leaving academia.

Many of us are also happy to be free from aspects of higher education that are downright toxic. Here I'm thinking of the job

2. Main, Prenovitz, and Ehrenberg (2018) show that job satisfaction levels for advanced-degree holders working in nonprofit and for-profit positions are higher across every category when compared with those in tenure-track and non-tenure-track positions (table 4).

market and its abusive labor practices; of departmental drama, intellectual squabbling, and questionable relationships; and of the tolerance for abusive behavior by advisors, chairs, and "talented" scholars that's taken for granted in many quarters of academia. The world beyond the ivory tower is hardly perfect, but it does a far better job of not pretending such conduct is normal or brushing it under the rug once it's been found out.

There are personal benefits, too. I always assumed that my best friends would come from the pool of people who loved studying the same academic material I did. But after a decade as a professional classicist, I could count the number of deep friendships I had from that world on one hand. The people I've met at my current company have been more outgoing, interesting, and nice than I ever could have imagined. Two years into that role, my close relationships numbered two dozen.

It's also been liberating to have an employer that makes my growth their priority. In academia, I was the only person responsible for my professional development. Today, I benefit from training courses, mentoring programs, and regular discussion of best practices. Each week, I have opportunities to sharpen old skills or acquire new ones—and have a group of supporters who proactively connect me to initiatives that can help me develop as a professional and leader. The extent of this support system no doubt stems from my company's large size and global scale, but other former academics I interviewed for this book also report finding much more collegial environments outside of higher education.

These benefits don't mean there aren't things we miss. David Engel still speaks fondly of the high he got from teaching. Others I know wish they could discuss thorny questions without deadlines or budgets putting an artificial stop on the conversation. No matter how happy you are in a new career, there's going to be something you're sad about losing. But the grass on this side of the fence really is greener, at least for those of us who think carefully about which way to jump before we start climbing out of the academic yard.

Looking Forward

If I've done my job in this book, you now know something of what lies beyond the event horizon of your career change. Whether your own path across it takes months or years, you're well equipped to find a job that fulfills your aspirations and know what it will take to adapt to a new environment.

When you settle into a new job, be realistic about the opportunity. You don't have to hold that position forever, and in fact most of us won't. Rather, we'll use it as a stepping-stone to new skills, new industries, and new ideas about the kind of work we want to pursue in our lives after academia.

Embrace this reality and use it to your advantage. If your first job doesn't turn out how you'd hoped, keep growing and look for new opportunities. Even if you love what you do next, periodically test the waters to see whether there's a job that you might enjoy more, that might pay a higher salary, or that might align more closely with your needs and desires as they evolve throughout your life. The transition out of academia is always the hardest. Subsequent career changes will be exponentially easier—and usually lead to greater rewards.

A Final Request

I'll end this book by asking for a favor. When you finish your career transition, you'll be walking proof of what someone with a PhD in your field can do in the "real world." This fact puts you on the front lines of changing common perceptions about what's possible with an advanced degree.

Whenever you can, advocate for other academics who end up traveling paths they didn't want or expect to walk. If someone asks you for an informational interview, make the time to do it. If they're looking for new contacts, connect them to people you know and coach them on how to build a network. This work isn't always convenient, and sometimes it's the last chore you want to do at the end of a long day. But if I know one thing, it's that you're going to receive more guidance, help, and support than you can imagine as you seek a new career. Once you've made it to the other side, I hope you'll join me in paying that kindness forward.

Action Items

1. Do something to celebrate! This isn't the end of a chapter—it's the start of one *you* get to write.
2. Email your networking contacts to let them know the good news and thank them for their help along the way.
3. After your first day on the job, update your LinkedIn profile so other academics can see what you're up to and reach out to you more easily

A NOTE ON THE TYPE

This book has been composed in Adobe Text and Gotham.
Adobe Text, designed by Robert Slimbach for Adobe,
bridges the gap between fifteenth- and sixteenth-century
calligraphic and eighteenth-century Modern styles.
Gotham, inspired by New York street signs, was designed
by Tobias Frere-Jones for Hoefler & Co.